Praise for *Soul Design*

"If you ever wondered about the origin of your soul and its various aspects, then Dr. Backman's book is a must-read! I have never read a more in-depth study and evaluation of the soul and its layers. From its original core to its build through various 'life experiences' here and in other spaces and times, *Soul Design* will give you a key awareness of who you truly are and why you have decided to come back to planet earth!"

—**JAMES VAN PRAAGH,** *New York Times* bestselling author of *Talking to Heaven*

"With wisdom and insight, breadth and depth, Dr. Linda Backman draws from her many client sessions to illuminate what we as souls are really doing here in the Earth school. For anyone who would like to draw back the curtain and peer behind the scenes into the underlying meaning and purpose of our Earth incarnations, this book is highly recommended."

—**ROBERT SCHWARTZ,** Between Lives Soul Regression hypnotist; author, *Your Soul's Plan* and *Your Soul's Gift*

"These uniquely brilliant soul origin stories have needed to be brought to the world's attention—especially as the world struggles to shift into a new age of expanded consciousness. Dr Linda brings this sacred knowledge to us with professionalism and a pure, unbiased, inquisitive process; it's like no other book on the subject.... It's brilliantly thought provoking and gives us new tools for navigating our lives on earth with purpose and compassion."

—**REV. SUE FREDERICK,** ordained unity minister, soul regression therapist, master numerologist, and founder of the Angelic Realm Ministry program

"Dr. Backman brings her more than thirty years of regression experience, sharing the soul-based memories and lessons that her clients bring forth during their sessions. She opens us to a deeper understanding of how each lifetime sets the stage for the next, including our soul families, relationships, and purpose. She also highlights conversations between our 3D selves and our 5D higher selves, in which our ultimate missions are revealed. Dr. Backman's *Soul Design* is a must-read for all of us seeking these answers."

—**REV. DR. VICTOR FUHRMAN,** interfaith minister and spiritual counselor, host and producer of OmTimes Radio's *Destination Unlimited*

"In her groundbreaking book *Souls on Earth,* psychologist and regressionist Dr Linda Backman laid bare decades of compelling data and case histories offering evidence of interplanetary souls—people who have lived on other worlds before incarnating here, and some for the very first time. In her latest book, *Soul Design*, she leads us one step farther on our evolutionary intergalactic journey by revealing how to integrate our immortal archetype with our current persona and original soul design. It is a riveting read from a pioneering author and teacher."

—**SANDIE SEDGBEER,** Talk TV / Radio host / OM Times Radio and founder of The No BS Spiritual Book Club

"A fascinating and comprehensive guide that dives deep into these profound questions. With her unique background as a psychologist and past-life regressionist, Dr. Backman offers a transformative understanding that can awaken your awareness and elevate your journey of self-discovery. In a time when clarity and spiritual growth are more essential than ever, this book serves as an invaluable resource for humanity. If you've ever wondered who you truly are, you must read this book. It's captivating, enlightening, and nearly impossible to put down."

—**KELLEE WHITE, LMFT**, psychotherapist, internationally recognized author of *Cracked Open*, YouTube Live host, and spiritual medium

"From one fellow therapist and regressionist to another, this masterpiece was beyond awakening, beautiful, and moving on a personal and professional level. Dr. Linda Backman, in her groundbreaking work, has provided a profound yet practical collection of client sessions with pointed evidence of the soul's awareness. This is a helpful read to support seekers to better understand themselves on a deeper soul level with laid out specific categories of the soul and our unique mission."

—**JACOB COOPER, LCSW,** author of *Life After Breath* and *The Wisdom of Jacob's Ladder*

Soul Design

About the Author

Dr. Linda Backman, EdD, licensed psychologist, has been in private practice since 1978. Dr. Backman is the author of *Bringing Your Soul to Light: Healing Through Past Lives and the Time Between* (Llewellyn Worldwide, 2009), *The Evolving Soul: Spiritual Healing Through Past-Life Exploration* (Llewellyn Worldwide, 2014), and *Souls on Earth: Exploring Interplanetary Past Lives* (Llewellyn Worldwide, 2018.) She also has graduate education and training in speech pathology, audiology, and special education. After experiencing the premature birth and death of her second child in 1972, Dr. Backman discovered the great need for more psychotherapists who are trained and devoted to working with those in grief. She cofounded an ongoing agency in Charlotte, North Carolina, dedicated to serving individuals and families who have experienced the death of children. In line with this work, she was asked to provide the commentary for the book *I Never Held You* by Ellen DuBois (DLSIJ Press, 2006).

Since 1993, Dr. Backman has guided innumerable individuals in regression hypnotherapy to access their past and between lives, also labeled as Higher Self. In this way, she helps people recognize who they are as souls throughout many lifetimes and when they are not incarnate. Regression hypnotherapy allows the client to understand their soul mission, soul progress, soul relationships, and much more. Dr. Backman's work today includes guiding regressions, speaking, writing, spiritual mentoring, and training others in the benefits of Soul Regression hypnotherapy in the United States and abroad. Dr. Backman is a frequent guest on spiritual podcasts, networks, and streaming services to educate others that we are an incarnate soul committed to aiding Humanity's evolution.

Dr. Backman studied and cotaught with Dr. Michael Newton, author of the seminal books *Journey of Souls* and *Destiny of Souls*. In 1997, Dr. Backman and her husband, Dr. Earl Backman, established The Ravenheart Center, a Mystery School dedicated to guiding individuals to discover their path as a soul. In addition, Dr. Backman founded the Ravenheart Soul Regression Collective, a network for regression therapists and for promoting awareness among the US and abroad public of the benefits and purpose of Regression Hypnotherapy.

The Backmans have been married for fifty-eight years and have two married children and three grandchildren.

For further information, please visit www.RavenHeartCenter.com or contact Dr. Backman at Linda@RavenHeartCenter.com.

A REGRESSIONIST'S GUIDE TO
Past Lives, Origins & Purpose

DR. LINDA
BACKMAN

WOODBURY, MINNESOTA

First Edition
First Printing, 2025

Cover design by Shira Atakpu

Library of Congress Cataloging-in-Publication Data
Names: Backman, Linda, author.
Title: Soul design : a regressionist's guide to past lives, origins & purpose / Dr. Linda Backman.
Description: First edition. | Woodbury, Minnesota : Llewellyn, [2025]
Identifiers: LCCN 2025007599 (print) | LCCN 2025007600 (ebook) | ISBN 9780738779201 (paperback) | ISBN 9780738779232 (ebook)
Subjects: LCSH: Spirituality. | Spiritual healing. | Regression (Psychology) | Soul.
Classification: LCC BL624 .B2957 2025 (print) | LCC BL624 (ebook) | DDC 133.901/35—dc23/eng/20250319
LC record available at https://lccn.loc.gov/2025007599
LC ebook record available at https://lccn.loc.gov/2025007600

Llewellyn Publications
A Division of Llewellyn Worldwide Ltd.
2143 Wooddale Drive
Woodbury, MN 55125-2989
www.llewellyn.com

Printed in the United States of America

Other Books by Dr. Linda Backman

Souls on Earth:
Exploring Interplanetary Past Lives

This book is dedicated to everyone who recognizes
life is a purposeful link on their soul's evolutionary chain
to make a difference in seemingly small yet grand ways.

Contents

Introduction

Imagine you and I are chatting with a cuppa in our hands. You ask me, "Linda, what led you to write another book? Why do you continue your work in soul regression after thirty years of witnessing what clients uncover in their sessions? Are you still learning more about the soul and reincarnation, or is it all repetitive?"

Past-life and between-lives soul regression is never dull or inconsequential. Week in and week out, clients speak of new insights. Once again, it was time to share numerous clients' soul journeys for anyone to read. My first book, *Bringing Your Soul to Light*, was published in 2009. *The Evolving Soul* emerged in 2014.

More than forty-seven years ago, I embarked on a professional journey as a psychologist. As some might say, I wanted to lend a hand to folks seeking to comprehend their thoughts, feelings, and passions. All too often, people are self-critical, labeling themselves as strange or not fitting into everyday culture. Conventional training as a psychologist prepared me to escort clients through the effects of their present-life biology and circumstances to take hold of actual details and release what no longer serves. Formal graduate training did not unlock and demystify who we are as a soul and why we are here now.

When my colleague passed away in 1993 and began communicating with me from the other side, I am sure my higher self and guides wondered how I would react. My life would never be the same, in a good way, as I wended my way the last thirty-two years to comprehend what I call soul essence psychology, specified by our incomparable soul design and life purpose. Each of us is a unique composite of three ingredients that begins with where our higher self resides, or soul origin, whether that's the earth's spiritual realm, the angelic realm that supports Source, or elsewhere in the celestial realm, such as planets, stars, and the like. Add in attributes of the happenings in our past lives, including skills, relationships, health issues, losses, and more. Your soul has an immortal archetypal quality that is purposeful, necessary, and evident in your past lives on this earth. Finally, our prebirth life contract, containing life's intentions today, is the final aspect of who we are.

Psychology is the study of our persona based on our current life. Soul essence psychology examines our current-life persona combined with our soul design, which is comprised of soul origin, past lives, and archetype. The absence of conscious awareness of our soul design is like flying an airplane that requires two engines, but only one is functional. For example, when you have an unmanageable fear of being on a ship in open water, yet nothing in life today explains such panic, the explanation likely arises from a past-life trauma.

Judging Your Thoughts, Feelings, and Spirituality

Every day, humans are taught to believe that our thoughts, fears, depression, attitudes, skills, interests, and the like originate exclusively from our genetic heritage and life experiences of today. When life provides minimal or no explanation of your characteristics, seek a broader awareness attached to your soul design. In the early 1990s, before I accepted reincarnation, our oldest child was scheduled to study abroad as an undergraduate. Months in advance of his travel, I began to experience ongoing anxiety night and day. Conventional therapy did not explain my struggle. Once regular communication began with him across the Atlantic, my agitation dissolved. Nearly ten years later, I discovered a past life where the soul of my son was my younger brother, whom I adored. As my sibling, he was abducted, and I lost him in that life.

Human nature makes us overly self-critical, often consisting of internal dialogue to "get over it." Realizing there is a logical explanation for seemingly nonsensical feelings and attitudes often lessens or eradicates our unwanted emotions. Soul essence psychology (SEP) serves as a road map, a prescription, and a decoding of who we are today, which we may otherwise mislabel as unbalanced. Reincarnation is the bedrock of SEP, and is exhibited by your past lives, soul origin, and archetype. Soul regression is the therapeutic tool that can divulge your soul characteristics and trajectory. When embodied, our higher self, or soul energy in the higher realm, provides the intuitive disclosure of who we are as a soul.

In my early years of guiding soul regression, most of my clients were earth-based souls (EBS) discovering earth past lives and their soul journey to evolve. Around 2006, it became clear that approximately half of my clients were interplanetary souls (IPS). In 2018, I was guided to offer details from exclusively IPS regression clients. With precision, I was intuitively informed that an entire book, *Souls on Earth*, was to be focused on the skills, challenges, and purpose of IPS on our planet. Such clients need support and awareness of their unique, valuable qualities.

Another shift happened in my client work around 2014 and continues until now. Soul regression in my current practice consists of 25 percent EBS, with the remaining 75 percent split between IPS and angelic realm souls (ARS). ARS are critical members of our human culture as they bear love and compassion in spades to humanity, which is considerably in need of such nonjudgmental energy. In this new compendium of client stories, you will come upon profound details of ARS, who discover the core of who and why they are on earth.

By design, my higher self and guides have positioned me to work with and discover unique skills and challenges of all three types of souls, or their soul origin. My intention is to remain in touch with my higher self and guides to recognize the incarnate souls I am to support, as well as to maintain my ongoing expansion as a soul regression therapist.

Two additional intentions underlie this new book. One is to demonstrate how your spiritual guides, perhaps your primary guide, is your higher self (HS). You receive conscious support and direction when you intuitively communicate with your HS. Additionally, I hope to show how learning the soul-level responsibilities of your HS provides insight into how your current life is tied to your soul agreements overall.

My career as a licensed psychologist was initiated over fifty years ago due to the premature birth and passing of our second baby. At the ripe young age of twenty-five, I endured a challenging pregnancy threatening miscarriage for four months. Adam, our second son, was born breathing and left his body within hours. Shock and depression ensued, leading me to seek psychotherapy. Discovering the benefits of therapy and the course of grief, I garnered a clear awareness of the complex emotions of loss. Years later, the intentional soul evolutionary objective of Adam's passing became apparent. Climbing the ladder of soul progression can be, but is not always, painful. The result of soul expansion is also freeing and de-light-ful.

Your Soul Design Road Map

I invite you to pick up your favorite beverage, perhaps with a pen and journal, and absorb each client and chapter as you revel in and examine your soul's journey. Only when you are willing to feel your feelings, trust your intuition, and *know* you're on a journey to evolve as a soul and impact humanity's elevation do you truly *know* your core self.

Consider this book a thought- and emotion-provoking tool. Whether your hunger to build a conscious framework to understand the soul, reincarnation, past lives, and life purpose is newly discovered or long standing, the revelations in the client regression narratives shared in this book will offer a road map. Trusting your intuitive insight as you navigate the upcoming stories will amplify your soul awareness, whether you choose to have a soul regression or not.

Each chapter closes with topical questions to examine. In addition, throughout the chapters, there are prompts to ask yourself about various matters, providing an illuminating assist as you unravel who you are as a unique embodied soul in life today with purpose. Come along on this intentional expedition to solidify your belief that we are immortal consciousness committed to evolving our soul and facilitating the evolution of humanity.

Dr. Linda Backman
Psychologist, Regression Therapist
Boulder, Colorado, 2025

CHAPTER ONE

Soul Essence Psychology Reflected in Soul Design

> You are a highly conscious soul and not all souls on this earth are. This doesn't mean you are better or worse than anyone else, just a different manifestation of energy and soul history. You may feel lonely at times because deep down you know that not everyone is like you. You may feel isolated because perhaps you hide your truest, biggest, brightest self from the world.
>
> —REBECCA CAMPBELL

In my life and the lives of my clients, key questions surface about who we are at a bedrock level and why we are incarnate now. SEP is the mode to illuminate our soul design based on past lives, soul origin, archetype, and life purpose. More than thirty years of guiding soul regression has gifted me with a treasury of soul-level apprehension. Each chapter will shed light on your essence as a soul. Begin to ponder and write or record. First, what relationship in life today suggests you are to balance past-life karma? Consider indications whether you are a soul who primarily incarnates and evolves on earth, a soul who does not regularly incarnate on earth and originated somewhere in the vast celestial realm, or a soul from the angelic realm. What experience have you had of grief and loss that is transformative? This chapter sets your journey in motion to reveal specifics about your foundational soul self.

What Is Soul Regression?

As a little girl, I wondered who I was. When I died, for example, would I go away forever? I struggled with this thought over and over. The idea that the me I knew as an eight-year-old would disappear made no sense. Unbeknownst to me, I had begun the process of tripping over myself. The soul-self part of me had started to seep into my conscious mind, though I had no understanding of why I was so sure that death was not the end. Perhaps you've had a similar experience as a child, while grappling with some tragic experience in your life or even just while lying awake in the stillness of the wee hours.

Over more than thirty years, I have guided thousands of soul regression clients. Let me explain a few basic notions that have been confirmed time and time again as clients share their unique experiences with me. You are more than your physical body and human personality. Your core energy is a spark of Source, created to gain wisdom and contribute to the evolution of humanity and the universe. Each time you embody on earth, your role is to progress individually and contribute to the transformation of human life. Before birth, with your spiritual guide(s), you drew up a life intention agreement.

Your soul has a mind of its own. By this, I mean that you incarnate with divine intelligence and intent, carrying with you your unwholesome, freewill past-life karmic choices that must be balanced by choosing more healthy behavior today. Your dharmic past-life accomplishments and skills will surface in support of your commitment to readjust prior immature actions.

Regression hypnotherapy is a mechanism or tool that allows an individual to access the memory of past lives and the client's HS that always exists in the spiritual realm of earth or beyond. It is an experience of utilizing relaxation to access our intuitive imagery, emotions, body sensation, smell, and cognitive knowing tied to our soul. During soul regression hypnotherapy, we function simultaneously in body and in the spiritual realm, experiencing our HS, that holographic counterpart of our deepest essence that resides permanently in spirit. During this encounter, we are gifted with the ageless and eternal knowledge of who we are as souls. Soul regression hypnotherapy is a powerful tool conducted by a trained practitioner utilizing specific breathing techniques, guided imagery, and other noninvasive means to guide the client into a natural state of relaxation, or trance hypnosis, conducive to accessing soul awareness.

I wish I could fully describe the opportunity to sit in the room during a soul regression session and witness the spontaneous descriptions that are my privilege and honor to hear. Still, as the therapist, I sigh with relief, knowing that it is not my job to guide these descriptions, nor do I determine the elements of past life experience or their significance to a client. The therapist is responsible for the session process, and the content is determined from a higher level of wisdom, the client's team of spirit guides and teachers. The information is received by and through the client, using intuition combined with an altered state of consciousness.

Thus, the client becomes their channel or conduit for the higher or soul self. As such, the substance of the session is not, I repeat, the responsibility of the hypnotherapist. Though an altered state of consciousness is induced, all hypnosis is self-hypnosis, and so the client is always in control of the process. The ability to receive intuitively and speak the details of lives one has lived before is an incredible experience for the client. So is the gift of receiving soul-level input relative to who and what we are and are intended to be. Many scientists believe we use the right temporal lobe of our brain to resonate with timeless energy fields, that we can use our human brain to access timeless, spaceless reality, which quantum physicists label as the nonlocal.

Still, it is difficult, if not impossible, to explain the literal and energetic mechanics of accessing soul memory, both in past lives and at the HS level. In essence, lessening the arousal or stimulation of our brain through regression hypnotherapy creates an altered state of consciousness that affords an opening to our intuitive or mystical processes.

The slower our brain wave activity, the more we are able to recognize or intuit the specifics of a past in which our soul resided in another body or a disincarnate state. In both past-life soul regression and between-lives soul regression, the process used to access these memories is a form of hypnosis. Hypnosis itself is about brain wave shift, also labeled as an altered state of consciousness, trance, or simply relaxation.

Frequently, clients ask how common it is to gain past-life and HS details during regression. My honest answer is that rarely do I work with a client who does not uncover soul-related details. Trust is a crucial attitude when you schedule a soul regression. As you traverse this book, I encourage you to keep a journal of realizations and emotions as you delve into your soul design road map.

Your Higher Self, Past Lives, and Life Purpose

Life is a continuous cycle—beginning at birth, ending upon death, and reviewed between lives in the spiritual realm. It starts anew with each upcoming incarnation, propelled by the soul's innate desire and inclination to progress in wisdom from one lifetime to the next. Your incarnate soul is a fragment, a sliver, of the totality of your divine energy or HS. The aspect of soul that is you comes from—and remains connected to—the celestial realm during your life on earth. Upon your physical death, the holographic portion of your soul that arrived before birth takes its leave and returns to the spiritual realm. Incarnations come and go, while soul consciousness is eternal.

Ask Yourself

What events or people in your life today suggest elements of your past lives and your intentions for soul evolution now?

A cardinal rule when I teach soul regression is that the therapist does not lead the witness. The therapist mustn't provide the client's intuitive content of past lives and their HS. Each client regression narrative presented in this book is spontaneous. My client Jonathan gives us a bird's-eye view of past-life completion and the natural return journey to the spiritual energetic setting of his HS.

JONATHAN: I Know Where I Am Supposed to Go

I have pneumonia. My young apprentice is mixing herbs and plasters. I do not want to die in the workroom and contaminate the herbs.

There are blankets all around me to keep me warm. I am having trouble breathing. I can't get enough air. My apprentice is with me. I die. It is just like a sigh. My apprentice is watching. She seems sad. She knows I am not entirely gone. I will help her sometimes. I will jog her memory.

Now I feel very floaty. I feel a nice pulsing. It is misty, foggy, and primarily white. I feel supported, but no one specific is with me. I am moving now. I know where I am supposed to go. There are more colors in the fog. Someone is here now. I feel at home. I feel welcome. I hear, "Glad you are back."

• • • • • • •

Often, my clients evaluate their past-life accomplishments as inadequate, only to have their guides explain their disagreement. Listen to Francesca as her past-life completes and she is given a choice to remain for a longer time before a new incarnation or forge ahead to continue her soul evolution and the evolution of humanity.

FRANCESCA: Talking with My Birth Mother

My husband and I are English. He is a British sea captain, and we live in India. He comes home and tells me we must return to England. We go home on a ship. It's horrible. We are caught in a storm; the ship goes down, and we both drown. I wanted to die in England and not like this.

My soul leaves the body of the woman I was. My guides tell me that I can remain in spirit to heal from the way I died or return to a life on earth very quickly. The husband in the past life is my husband of today.

My guides tell me that I can be with the soul of my past-life husband again. So, I chose to return to my new present-life embodiment without taking time to heal from the way I died.

My guide tells me that because of the drowning and my adoptive mother's personality of frequent fear and panic, it is hard not to feel anxiety.

Now, the soul of my birth mother comes forward. She tells me that she was ashamed of being pregnant at such a young age. She tells me that I was a love child, but she was afraid she was not ready to raise me.

My guides tell me that because I was given up for adoption, I was able to help my adoptive mother, who needed to learn how to love a child.

Helping my adoptive mother to heal is one of my commitments now. I will be able to release the anxiety because I understand how I died in the past life is related. I am accomplishing my soul intentions today.

••••••••

Francesca receives clear-cut explanations for some of the most profound questions in her regression. First, what caused our death in the past life may linger and impact a future life experience. Francesca's anxiety in her current life is partially explained by the trauma she still carries from drowning. When we complete a life, our soul transitions into spirit with the opportunity to resolve the emotions surrounding how we died. If emotional energy tied to the dying circumstance remains in our soul DNA, symptoms of the past will present to be healed in today's incarnation.

Second, we always have free will to mend elements of a past incarnation during the time between lives. Francesca opted to reincarnate again with the soul of her past-life spouse in relatively short order. In life today, imbalanced energy or karma caused by unsettled past-life events will arise, requesting to be understood and laid to rest.

Third, in soul regression, a loved one in spirit can communicate to provide critical information. Francesca's birth mother, directed by her guides, explains why she opted to give her baby up for adoption. Francesca has the choice to release herself from the pain of her birth mother and be free rather than holding someone else's emotions.

Finally, two essential elements of information about Francesca's adoptive mother come to light: the frequent fear and panic of her personality style and her need to learn how to love a child, which provided a large amount of explanation for Francesca. This client, in her sixties, can grasp and detach from a previous mystery. Baggage held in Francesca's soul memory is obliterated energetically through shoring up her guides and taking steps to acknowledge emotion, letting it go and building awareness of her life purpose.

Gifts and Challenges Revealed in Your Life Purpose

Each incarnation is filled with preplanned intentions, not simply one purpose. Susan's regression displays a vital gift she bestows: supporting others to know they matter. Consider the value of someone in your life who conveys you are worthy.

SUSAN: Bridging the Knowledge Gap with Love

As a soul, everyone has a purpose. I am no different. We are all here to help and influence others. Each soul adds a particular influence. My job is to link, making souls feel that they belong and have a reason and a purpose for being here.

It is all about love, no matter what. I am to join people together so they do not feel alone. To do so, I listen in earnest to people. I become their friend and give them a feeling of belonging. I help them with realizations and answers. Then I move on. I always leave behind the interaction that I have had with someone.

I am to talk to people who are unsure and unhappy. Many of these people have phobias and problematic attitudes. I cannot stop what happens to people. Often, they must go through difficult experiences. I have not had life in this sphere for hundreds of lives.

I am here to experience this type of life and gain a better understanding. I am to influence others unobtrusively. I came to earth to experience what pain feels like. I did not know what pain was before; there is pain in many different forms, and it is caused in many ways.

It is my life lesson to gain this knowledge and return it to the angels. The angels know there is pain on earth. Yet, more angelic souls must be prepared to withstand the intensity and struggles of human life.

I thank them (my spiritual team) for being there and allowing me this realization, this life, and this precious learning experience.

They tell me that I cannot cure all ills. I am not meant to be able to resolve all pain. The biggest thing of all is love.

•••••••

Susan recently retired from the computer industry. She has spent much of her working and private life talking with and supporting those she contacts. On the surface, her life does not appear to powerfully reflect her life purpose, as described by her spiritual team. Nonetheless, like many other souls, she has come into body with a profoundly spiritual intention; guiding others to believe that they are not alone, they fit in, and they are here on earth for a distinct reason is inexplicably essential. If we think our existence serves no purpose, we will likely feel bereft, like a boat floating in the water without an engine.

Susan assists many people whom others might avoid or misunderstand. Suspending judgment, she offers love where others would be critical and withhold it. However, understanding the trauma of others' lives is Susan's cup of tea. Her task on this planet is just the opposite. In other words, Susan's mandate for her present life is to understand and comprehend the depth of pain many people face and carry the energetic imprint of that complexity and difficulty back to souls in spirit.

Numerous regression hypnotherapy sessions have demonstrated that the job of certain incarnate souls is to facilitate learning both in the spiritual realm and on earth. These souls may not have incarnated on earth in a very long time, if ever. The density of the earthly laboratory where we gain soul development can be intensely painful and too complicated to endure. And so, for adequate coordination and understanding between the spiritual realm and earth, particular souls have agreed to serve as gatherers of awareness, bringing such knowledge to the higher levels of the universe.

Ask Yourself

Are my current-life intentions primarily focused on balancing past-life karma, or am I absorbing the challenges of human life to prepare more experienced souls for earth's incarnation?

Soul Essence Psychology and Soul Design Reveal Gifts and Challenges

Early human intelligent life, as embodied souls, has existed on earth for over a million years. Actual civilization began approximately five thousand years ago in the Indus River Valley, where India and Pakistan meet, in Mesopotamia at the Tigris-Euphrates River System, and in Egypt. To expand your grasp on the essential psychology of your soul design, consider three possibilities of your soul origin and where your HS exists. Ninety-five percent of humanity comprises EBS, who begin their gradual journey to evolve on earth as young souls at the kindergarten stage of development. EBS incarnate over and over on earth, gaining evolution through prebirth agreement and karmic, freewill choice of action to expand. Our HS is always in the spiritual energy tied to our soul origin. For EBS, our HS resides in the earth's spiritual realm at an energetic frequency beyond our planet. Jane, in the following client example, reviews how EBS work together in soul pods and select souls to serve in upcoming life roles.

JANE: Insights During the Soul Regression

I am moving through the clouds. There are cloud shapes around me. I am back in my pod (soul group) to be known as I am. I feel accepted, not judged. There are seven to nine people (souls). There are two to three interacting with me. They say, "It is good to have you back." They all say hi.

Now, I need to be debriefed. The three go with me. I arrive where my past life will be processed. There are three entities inside, and we go over things I had done in my past life. I did not choose the right person to marry. I let my head get turned by a pretty girl. The woman I should have married was plain but solid. However, there is no completely wrong choice.

What I took away from my choices was to pay better attention to my gut.

It can affect others also if I need to pay attention. That life was about handling disappointment and learning to make the best of it.

I am taken to a waterfall, and my guides tell me I must wash off the previous life. There is an energy mist. It feels good to breathe it in. I needed to release something from the dying in that life. It smells good, like alyssum, a honey smell. Now, the waterfall runs clear. I am done, they tell me.

I go to a room that is open to nature, and they guide me to practice trusting my intuition. Then, I will make better choices and be in balance. This is different from my beginning pod. Three of us from my original soul group joined this specialized group. Later, there will be an even smaller cohort.

My group now deals with understanding the basics of healing to help others advance. As a soul, when you reach a higher degree of evolution, you work with equally advanced souls. Victor, my son, is one member of this group. There are other groups nearby, like this group.

The different small groups interact with each other so that when you put together a life, you might choose from different groups near you. You can choose someone from a different small group to serve their needs or yours. My husband and son from life today are both in my group. They play with energy like I do.

The teacher for our group stops by. She has us play with emotions, like playing with energy. Emotions can help us learn and experience. Emotions can be unpleasant. We are to move at a slower pace so that we will see the nuances. We will miss the importance of the emotion if we move too fast. I am told that stress can affect my health, so I am to go slow and pay attention to what is essential. They want me to approach most of life like a play.

• • • • • • •

Jane is the recipient of powerful advice on how to focus on life. We are to listen to our gut and not have our heads turned by beauty. If someone or something lacks outer loveliness it may indicate that the person or life is solid and robust. If we follow our emotions and take time to examine things, we are likely to discover what is of more excellent value in life. Including play is critical.

Jane's soul regression content identifies her as an EBS, attributable to the size of her soul pod and how she has evolved to work with a smaller group of souls. IPS and ARS almost always have small soul pods, numbering approximately four. Plus, IPS and ARS do not progress to an even smaller work group. Jane is an EBS providing details about advancing from our original soul family into a synchronized smaller soul group. To recap, as an EBS, we begin our soul's journey by interacting with our soul pod, a group of souls numbering approximately eight to fifteen. The members of this initial soul group advance at differing rates of soul development, leading to subgroups forming. Eventually, we work with three to five selected members of this team as an advanced soul cohort with a designated task.

Souls on Earth: Soul Origin Home Settings

If you are an EBS, your soul originates in, and your HS resides at an energetic frequency tied to, the earth's spiritual realm. If you are an IPS, your soul arises from a location in the vast celestial realm, such as a planet, star, interdimensional energy, or spacecraft. Last, if you are an ARS, your soul begins and remains in the setting where angels support the high frequency known as God, Source, or Manu. EBS become highly familiar with life in an earth body because of their nearly exclusive terrestrial incarnation.

Absorb now an IPS whose soul regression reveals her primitive past life of teaching men nonabusive action. Upon completing this life, Iris's soul energy integrates with her HS on a spacecraft, and she discovers that her fundamental role is the healthy balance of earth's oceans to sustain aquatic life. An IPS's native environment is a healthy culture somewhere in the celestial realm. Commonly, my IPS clients are wise yet challenged by various health issues, from simple to complex, such as allergies and autoimmune disorders. In addition, IPS do not have vast human experience, which leads to social and financial distress.

IRIS: An IPS Devoted to Fixing Male Behavior and Oceanic Conditions

I'm a man outside in a dry, hot place. I have light-colored leather shoes and a simple one-piece leather garment. I'm wearing a bone necklace. I'm a primitive human with a long beard.

I've been walking for a long time. My family is far away. I was traveling with someone, but they died. It was a man who knew the way, but I do not. It's getting cold because the season is changing. I don't have enough clothes. There's no way to get back home because of the cold. I find a small cave, but it's not warm. I try to survive, but I don't have enough food. I lean against a rock and die.

It takes me a long time to die because I'm very strong. Now, I'm traveling and am in a thin layer of white. I feel bad about leaving that life because I had two children. I tell them goodbye with my energy. I kiss them on their heads. I wasn't ready to go. My wife feels my energy and knows I've died. One of my children is the soul of my brother of today.

I'm in pink-purple energy. I'm going upward, and there are stars everywhere. It's quiet and peaceful. I see a spaceship that is like a glowing blue dish. Someone is waiting for me outside the spacecraft. They don't look human and have a soft green shape.

They take me into the spacecraft and close the door. The souls are welcoming. They take me to a small blue pool. I'm floating in detoxifying minerals and can see the stars. I feel I'm female energy now, but not physical. Time is different, and I stay for a long time. No one measures the time where I am.

Now, a being with its arm around my shoulder guides me out of the pool and walks me somewhere. I feel joyful. I'm still in the spaceship that watches over the planets. The being, Jeff, is like a peer or big brother. It's a big ship, and all the beings are busy.

We walk into the control room, and six beings greet me. They have different jobs and put their work on autopilot so we can sit down and talk. I put on a blanket that holds my energy. We communicate telepathically, eye to eye. They tell me I'm doing a good job and are proud of me. I helped my community in the past life as a nice man.

As that man, I helped ensure that men were not abusive. I taught men not to use their strength against each other. Evolving men's behavior is tied to humanity's evolution. It was not my fault that I got lost because I was looking for more food.

Now, I need time to rest and don't need to do anything immediately. Jeff takes me to a cabin and helps me settle back into the ship. He gives me something to drink. After I rest, they bring me back to the control room to get back to work. It is so good to be back. Our spacecraft monitors how one planet can throw the weather off for other planets. Our job is to bring related planets back into harmony.

Also, the temperature of the oceans on earth must be regulated to sustain life. My job is tied to the oceans. I direct a team of feminine-energy souls that incarnate on earth to balance the energy of the oceans. My type of body where I come from is made to live in the ocean. Now, I am on the planet where my fellow souls reside to check on them. They are welcoming and greet me with respect.

I am an IPS. Some of my work is done from the spacecraft, but my home location is this giant planet where I've gathered with my fellow souls whose role is to support the healthy energy of earth's oceans. I am checking to be sure they are not overextending themselves since they must stay balanced.

I am back to the spacecraft and am with Jeff. We're looking over many planets. I'm told my life purpose is to be a leader among women since I have unique skills to communicate literally and intuitively. I am to help dissolve the patriarchy. Jeff is not my primary guide. My guide looks like an old woman with white hair. Her name is Clara. She wants me to be sure to have fun and feel joy.

• • • • • • •

Iris's regression detail is revelatory when characterizing an IPS. First, the past life early in human culture exhibits men needing guidance and the ongoing contemporary necessity for men to avoid abusive action. Iris's early human life closes to reveal she is an IPS who, like many IPS, has been incarnating on earth for a long time. A spacecraft is where Iris accomplishes tasks, like a human who goes to the office. IPS often have a unique appearance that is not at all human. Cleansing is the first essential task to release the challenging energy of earth life before Iris can continue duties on the ship.

Critical aspects of Iris's soul and responsibilities shed light on how IPS aid the earth and beyond. For my client, her HS and human self-focus on balancing the ocean's chemistry is a crucial activity. Consider the revelation for my client, since she has spent years donating to humanitarian ocean-protecting causes. Last, Iris carries an additional undertaking on earth, which is to speak for the needs of women ignored by the patriarchy.

IPS are gifted and yet challenged to function in the human world. Each IPS stems from its natural environment in the vast celestial realm and has native qualities. Natural features for an IPS include being emotion focused, thought focused, nature focused, and animal focused, with no romantic partners, no children, and no other characteristics specific to the home setting. Due to a lack of experience functioning in a human body and environment, IPS often struggle to cope and have allergies, digestive disorders, social anxiety, ADHD, autism, financial instability, and more.

Turning now to the third type of soul that incarnates on earth, although infrequently: an ARS who conveys a deep and genuine energy of love and compassion for all living things, almost to a fault. ARS must be cautious not to give so much of themselves that they deplete their resources.

JANELLE: A Teacher of the Open Heart

I am inside an endless space that is ethereal and cloudlike. There is color here with the gradation of green and white light. It is soft and flowing. I'm walking through it. I'm alone, and it's peaceful.

I'm in an observation mode of total peace. I'm in an atmosphere that I've never felt before. I am experiencing the location of my HS. My spiritual guide is above and slightly behind me. I feel a partnership with my guide, who is wearing a flowing robe. My guide's name is Michael, and he has wings.

Michael tells me I'm on the right path. Now I feel a dear friend who recently passed who is with Michael. My friend, Stash, tells me that he and I teach others they are perfect and complete. Stash continues to support me from the higher realm and explains we are educators who inspire and guide others. My friend is an ARS.

Michael explains he is an archangel and my primary guide. Michael says that my soul energy has wings. I am a humble and modest soul because I know there is a power greater than just me. I feel tremendous gratitude for being a piece of that whole. My wisdom is born out of experience that flows through me. I have had more than twenty-five earth lives.

I am an ARS. My purpose is to mirror the image of the divine. With grace and integrity, I can bring forward the principles of life with abundance for all to realize. I will model the teachings created by another friend who has passed, Katie. One of my unique abilities and commitments is to partner with dear ones in the higher realm whose teachings on earth have supported many to evolve.

With my husband and children, I am to love them just how they are and allow them their timetable of self-discovery. It is their journey. I am to dig deeper into my discoveries and not the discovery of others. Archangel Michael reminds me to have an open heart.

• • • • • • •

So many humans don't realize their perfection and completeness, which explains why the higher realm guides ARS to earth and continues to expand the numbers, though they are only 1 to 2 percent of humanity. ARS tend to stand out with their expansive kindness and lack of judgment. Janelle must embrace her core of gentleness and caring while not viewing herself as too soft. Some ARS are guided by an archangel, while others receive support from another ARS. Often, I caution an ARS client to be sure to care for themselves and not give all their energy away. Janelle's regression demonstrates how our loved ones are on their correct course, as we love them and allow them their personal decisions.

Ask Yourself

Do I know someone who is exceedingly nonjudgmental and accepting of all others?

Soul Essence and Design: Relationships, Loss, and Guides

Your soul essence and design has underpinnings of support and direction, with intentional themes and passions. Your daily life reveals preplanned ups and downs created to advance your soul evolution and your contribution to humanity's advancement. People who come into your life, endings that occur, and ceaseless directive counsel are clues that manifest why you are embodied now with never-ending spiritual oversight in life today.

ROY: Anger and Cancer—the Connection

Roy is in his sixties and has been challenged by two different types of cancer for more than four years. He lives alone in a secluded area and is continually fraught with anger and distress over the materialism and surface mentality of life on earth. As you absorb Roy's past life, notice his unrelenting anger, grief over losing his wife, and physical trauma that ended his life. Life events and circumstances are preplanned. Of crucial importance is the fact that we have complete control of how we react to life's events, whether with despair and frustration or acceptance and transformation.

It's daytime, and I'm out in the forest. It's a lovely, warm day; I'm wearing just a loincloth and moccasins. I'm Native American, with long black hair pulled back and tied with a strip of leather. I'm a young adult man, bare chested. I'm out hunting and love being in the forest. I'm carrying my bow and a quiver with arrows. Now I can hear men in the distance, Spanish men. They wear armor. I'm lying low and hiding.

Where I am is like a tropical jungle. The men go by with their strange metal armor rattling, but they don't see me. Now they've captured me. These Conquistador-looking guys surround me. They're restraining my muscular body. They speak a language I don't understand. I'm angry and spit in their faces. One of them backhands me. I'm enraged. One of them pulls out a long knife. He stabs me in the throat. I slump to the ground and die. My soul slips out through my back. Now I feel like I'm flying; I'm a better man than they. I don't want to leave my wife. She is the same soul as my ex-wife of today. I need to apologize for judging her so harshly. She tells me that it's okay.

I wish I'd been able to warn my people about these invaders because they will cause so much trouble. I hear Jesus say, "Father, forgive them, for they know not what they do." This was a beautiful country before these Spaniards arrived. They just wanted to hunt us, steal from us, and show us no respect. They wanted us to convert to their beliefs.

In my current life, I want to escape civilization; I don't think like the modern world. My guides tell me that I was a good soul in my past life. These Europeans should not have done what they did. I had a lot of anger toward these bastards. Now I see they killed my wife and son; they burned our village. I am Chickasaw; it's 1541 with DeSoto.

•••••••

Roy's past life shows up in his life today in various ways. Unresolved past or current anger can eat away at our core, potentially causing emotional and physical challenges. At times, we complete a past life and pass on without resolution of the trauma, unable to control our past-life events. Roy of today has chosen an escape mode to remove himself from everyday culture. His guides found it imperative to illuminate his lack of resolution of his past life.

Roy can release his deep upset with conscious awareness of past-life happenings. Spiritual guides and intuitive direction are available to us when we are open to receiving them. Past-life loss can live within our HS energy until we accept what occurred and let it go. A key element to reaching higher levels of soul evolution is to face loss and grief and allow our painful feelings.

Next, Rachel demonstrates how we are expected to incorporate the transformation available to us when we assimilate our life tragedies, let go of anger, and climb higher on the ladder of acceptance.

RACHEL: Speaking Up for Justice with Love

I'm inside, and men are talking. A lantern lights the room. I look like a pilgrim, with long dark hair, a pilgrim-type hat, and those black shoes with a buckle. I'm a middle-aged male, and it feels like New England. We're early settlers in America.

We're having a meeting, and a document is being discussed. I will sign because I don't want to get in trouble. I'm not enthusiastic about it. This is some declaration before the Declaration of Independence. I think it is tied to William Penn. This is after the Mayflower. There are only men in the room, no women. This is an active insurrection that I don't want to get into because I don't think we can win. Still, we must take this step.

Now I'm being hanged. I get in trouble for this kind of thing a lot. I stand up for what is right, and I'm being punished. I am more intelligent than the people who hanged me, but I lack the wisdom to shut up. The time was not right to speak up. I've died and am rising out of the back of my body. I've been killed a lot for standing up for what is right. I've gotten in trouble because I speak out for justice in my past lives. In some cases, my death has assisted others to speak their truth, which is good.

I sense a man, a guide, meeting me; he says, "Well done." He's wearing a white robe and calls himself John. He tells me I usually don't fit in and am not a joiner. He says that I need to forgive the world for its ignorance. I can forgive when I'm not in body, but when I'm incarnate, I'm angry. I need to stay awakened when in body; I'm told I am eternal love, light, and wisdom. I succumb to my anger. This creates illness in my body. John tells me that it's okay, that no one is perfect.

I sense a globe of white light. The light scans me like an eraser that removes scars but not memories. I've fought for what's right in many lives and been punished. I ask how I can forgive others for what they do. I'm told that love is the only way. I'm told that ignorance causes behavior that leads to a lack of unity.

I'm told I've forgotten who I am: a teacher. My body, in many lives, has been scarred. I must release my anger and forgive. This is the only way to heal my body from the health issues I've been experiencing. My life purpose is to find joy in adversity. I am to dispel ignorance and suffering. We are all in this together.

•••••••

John, Rachel's guide, paints a clear picture of her frequent past-life purpose: being willing to serve as an outsider while speaking for justice and tolerating ignorance. Love is the medicine to apply in the sight of ignorance. Rachel must accept that she is an experienced soul who sometimes dies to advance her soul's evolution and progress humanity.

The words *adversity, joy, ignorance, suffering,* and *forgiveness* together reflect a clear picture of how life naturally happens and is to be accepted day-by-day. Life on earth ascends and descends with related emotions, all essential to strengthening our core, seeking soul and humanity's evolution. As a soul, Rachel has embodied numerous times to stand up for what is right, even in the face of punishment and death. In modern times, consider the notion of death not tied to physical passing. At times, we must stand our ground, holding fast to our belief in just action, no matter the attitude of others. Allowing our fears to die opens a window to enhanced emotional strength and opportunity. A changemaker who follows their heart is essential to move humanity forward. William Penn founded Pennsylvania for religious freedom in the late 1600s.

Ask Yourself

What do the words *joy* and *adversity* mean to you?

In Summary

SEP elevates our perspective of who we are today—in mind, body, spirit, attitude, knowledge, and passion—to a level of knowing ourselves in ways we may not have expected. In past lives, where and when you lived gives rise to an affinity for locations and eras of time. Skills such as music, painting, mapmaking, and oratory, or passions like herbs, travel, astrology, and caring for children, all suggest who you were in prior embodiment. An intense avoidance of childbearing, romantic partnerships, travel by ship, and medical practitioners with no explanation in present life all suggest trauma in lives past.

Anxiety or exhaustion that seems to have no apparent cause may stem from past lives. Your HS has agreed to higher realm coordination and evolutionary responsibility, seeking earth's transformation to a healthier function. During times when your HS is engaged with earnest upgrade activity at the soul level, agitation and sleep disturbance may result. By trusting your intuition, you can tune in to your HS to gain input about current happenings.

Past-life experience and the role of our HS provide two elements of your soul design. To expand the makeup of your soul design, an essential component is whether you are an EBS, IPS, or ARS. Locating your soul's home location and whether you've had innumerable or few lives on earth points you toward grasping your unique skills and challenges.

Think about your soul design like a jigsaw puzzle with pieces coming together gradually to form a whole image. Learning to live with and transform beyond grief tied to the passing of a loved one, as well as a significant loss of home, job, romantic relationship, and more, demonstrates to our HS and guides that we're committed to the path of evolution. Our soul and humanity reveal themes of soul expansion that are essential to maturation as an individual soul and an earthly culture. Examples encompass not becoming a victim of grief and loss, including loss of normal human function such as eyesight, hearing, walking, and more. In addition, a balance of human equality tied to gender, sexual orientation, ethnicity, and the like must occur in our past lives and today's lives.

We souls have a primary spiritual guide who is always with us. Our guide or team of guides underpins the specifics of our upcoming-life blueprint. As we trust our intuition, the door to our life purpose—whether it's income-producing work, life partners, parenting, and more—is divulged. In the upcoming chapters, absorb more revelatory details from client soul regressions. As you put pen to paper in your journal, draw on your natural flow of thoughts and feelings to reflect on the points shared below and answer the homework questions. Ask your guides for intuitive input and capture the content in your journal.

Things to Think About

- Your life today likely includes one, or more than one, person with whom you have agreed to alter your past-life behavior and heal your relationship.
- IPS usually were children who were fascinated with the night sky.
- A significant loss in your life was designed to elevate your soul evolution.

Homework to Illuminate the Essence of Your Soul Design

1. What is your greatest challenge or joy in life that may reveal your life intentions?
2. Do you believe you've been embodied on earth many times or few?
3. What fear have you overcome that is likely tied to a past life?

CHAPTER TWO

Soul Power Revealed in Higher Self and Human Self

> You have a purpose, and your higher self will see to it that you carry out that purpose, whether it's done in a few hours or a hundred years, whether you do it kicking and screaming all the way or having a delightful time.
>
> —SERGE KING

Often ignored in spiritual discussion is our HS. Whether we are incarnate or not, our soul energy, or HS, is in the higher realm. HS is always one of our spiritual guides, and sometimes our primary guide. Give thought to signs from your HS; they are present and leading you forward. As we have prebirth and ongoing additions to our life contract, our HS is responsible for aiding humanity's evolution. Your actions on earth relate directly to your HS's role in spirit, and vice versa. Reflect consciously and intuitively on the reciprocal support between you and your HS.

There is a great dichotomy in life: our soul dwells at a higher frequency called the spiritual realm, while our human self is our embodied soul on earth. When we begin a new incarnation, we contain a holographic slice of the totality of our soul energy. To understand this, think about a pie that you cut into portions. The portion of pie on your human plate is tethered to the remainder of your soul, the HS, which resides in the spiritual realm.

Soul Essence's Higher Realm Location and on Earth

Viability at birth happens because we have soul energy within us. Our HS, which comprises all the evolution we've gained from life to life, is constantly available. Here's the critical concept we must accept: our HS serves as a spiritual guide in everyday life for each of us. Think of your HS as that benevolent teacher who knows you well and is present to offer advice and direction.

Your HS connotes the power of your soul energy. Remember that your soul essence includes past lives, soul origin, soul archetype, and life contract, reflected in the skills and intentions of your present life. Think of it like a car. Your HS is the engine, and the car's body is you. When you look in the mirror, you see this life reflection, and unseen with human eyes is your HS standing behind you.

Intuitive communication is a skill and a gift of human nature. Some of us are born with our intuitive radio turned on loud and clear. Others, like me, must learn to tune our awareness to intuitive reception later in life. Your ability to recognize sixth sense communication may be through imagery, emotions, body sensation, or thought.

Your passport to receiving HS input is to trust your intuitive reception mode and practice it. Ask a close friend to work with you for an exercise and tap into how that friend is doing. Next, check out your gut-level hunch about your friend. Don't expect to be 100 percent accurate; no one ever is. Valid intuition is your goal.

We begin this chapter about HS with the regression experience of Nadine, a sixty-year-old real estate broker. During her preliminary interview, she wanted to learn two things from her session: How could she reconnect with her past lives? What block kept her from sensing soul-level guides and teachers on her own? As her session unfolded, she received a glimpse of the radiant nature of her HS, that astonishing presence that is her core. Nadine's account opens as she dies in her past life and travels onward into the spiritual realm.

NADINE: A Glimpse of the Higher Self

My soul goes whirling off. It is like a spiral dance as I go up into the light. I am free and expanding. There is a sense of awe as I reach out and connect with the energy field of my soul, guides, and Source. I feel ecstatic and complete. Now I must go to be processed. Beings will guide me.

Angelic beings take away the old residue. I have come away from a life that had so much responsibility. Now, I am in the eternal location of my soul. I do not need to do anything just now. I must let go of needing always to do something. It is enough just to be.

Nadine takes flight like an airplane lifting off the runway and tucking in its wheels. Descriptors such as *free*, *expanding*, and *awe* barely scratch the surface to portray the sense of freedom out of body. Soul regression affords us access to our HS, our soul energy that is not held within a dense corporeal container.

Nadine paints a picture of the freedom she feels as pure soul, released from the confines of density. Being processed usually indicates two happenings: time for rest, cleansing, and rejuvenation as needed, and a high-level conference with your guidance team to evaluate the life just completed. Whether you are satisfied with your accomplishments in the life just completed or not, you must be forthcoming. Your wise teachers insist you explain how you might have behaved differently.

Be-ing and do-ing during a lifetime must be in balance. As Nadine's guides suggest, she is to take time to chill. For many of us, it is challenging to accept that we have done enough. Each time we arrive on earth, we have a new life plan that includes karmic cleanup and brings forth what we have learned from previous lives. Some of our incarnations are more do-ing and some not. An alternative life plan can be one in which we have accomplished what was needed, and in the future it is time to enjoy the fruits of our labor and have a tranquil environment.

Ask Yourself

Can I take fifteen minutes daily to relax, breathe, and invite my HS in? Trust that you can hear your soul level. Even though you may think you are making up what is coming through, keep going—you are *not* fabricating the communication from your HS. Nadine continues:

> *I start growing. It is like I've been resting like a seed in the ground. In this place, I can grow as big as possible. I need to reconnect with my HS and find out where I belong in a group of souls. All I must do is put my mind to it.*
>
> *These beings live in a mountain range. My teacher, Leo, who died in my current life, is there. This is a group of ascended masters that includes Saint Germaine and the Brotherhood. I am part of this group soul with the mission to bring consciousness and light to open people's awareness.*
>
> *Why can we not make more of an impact on earth? We forget who we are. There is a downward pull on this level, on earth, where we need love and acceptance. Therefore, we adapt. It is easy to have self-doubt and hard to maintain our soul experience.*

•••••••

Departing a body as simply soul energy upon completing a life and leaving the confines of humanness is always described as surprisingly expansive and calming. As her soul rises from the third dimension through the astral plane to the fifth dimension and beyond, Nadine indicates her awareness of returning to her HS and the group of souls with whom she works closely.

My years of guiding soul regressions have led me to conclude that Nadine is an evolved soul who primarily incarnates on earth (EBS), because Master Saint Germaine and the Brotherhood primarily guide experienced souls who come to earth. EBS are almost always embodied in earth bodies, which affords them more excellent experiences within humanity than an IPS or ARS. *Ascended master* designates an EBS who may still, or may no longer, incarnate.

Ask Yourself

Why can I not make more of an impact on earth? Consider the following explanations that Nadine receives, plus do more deciphering of what gets in our way of evolving human culture. First, many of us lack sufficient love and acceptance, including self-acceptance. Being in touch with your humanity and HS means you never lose sight of needing to sustain your human life while always knowing you are a soul who agreed to be embodied at this time. Growing and evolving your soul and helping humanity evolve is essential.

> *This is a mythic realm in the mountain, where there are symbols that are a powerful language to represent consciousness and the alchemy of energy. We can create symbols to help us remember who we are and resonate with the deepest sense of the universe. I need to go deeper into my knowledge of consciousness. I have pushed away this realm's images because the material world's stress is too great. I want to resonate with the human world, so I need to remember my knowledge of the greater universe.*

•••••••

Nadine clearly expresses the challenge of recognizing her unending attachment to the higher realm while functioning in body on earth. Living our intentional life on earth contains two obligations: living daily as a human being while never losing sight of the knowledge that we are a soul, and having a human experience with purpose.

The spiritual realm is as real as the fingers on your hand. How we recognize the presence of our HS, our spiritual guide, and the souls of our loved ones comes into focus through a myriad of energetic avenues. Invite yourself to fully trust that symbols—such as the seasonal light on the stones at Stonehenge or crop circles that arise overnight—are energetic messages. The speaker in your home that turns on spontaneously, the license plate on the car in front of you that has meaningful letters and numbers, and other examples relate to Nadine's higher realm comments. The material world can cloud our acceptance; there is more than our human eye can see.

Please remember that your HS guides you to advance in your life on earth as you support your HS fully functioning in her role as a soul in the spiritual realm. Each of your incarnations contains a holographic portion or aspect of your soul energy, and what remains in the higher realm is your HS. Your HS works in the higher realm while you are accomplishing things on earth.

What you accomplish in the higher realm is as important as how you live your life intentions on earth. I implore you to know that you matter on earth, and your HS is crucial in the spiritual realm.

The questions Nadine brings to her soul regression session indicate she is spiritually very aware. She realizes she has constricted herself and forgotten who and what she is as a soul. Her session allows her to renew her grasp of the core of her being. Traveling to share time with her advanced group in the mountains gives her extra perspective on the knowledge and capability she commands. Her HS comprehends the minuscule forms of energy in nature and can also recognize consciousness's symbology or energetics.

Using Intuition to Hear Your Higher Self

Third-dimensional reality is what many view as the totality of life. Everyday life exists in the material realm of our linear mind, the world of bills, daily chores, appointments, and so on. All too often, we become identified with our bodies, our minds, and our daily routines and rituals in this dense energy space we call earth.

Higher consciousness, the realm of divinity or spirituality, tugs at our deeper awareness. Sometimes, a dream will indicate that a loved one who is no longer physically present is near. The birth of an infant, when a new lifetime begins, reminds us of the miracle of life we call reincarnation.

As our current life or incarnation progresses, many of us recognize the strain of grappling with events from a grounded, earthly, and logical perspective only. Life's traumas, particularly those related to loss, sometimes make no sense at all. Death, divorce, health issues, jobs, relationships, abuse, and other such concerns require a deeper, more spiritually focused explanation. Predominantly, what we face in our human lives is tied to who we are as a soul and how we are to evolve in life today. For example, when your beloved spouse of five years passes at age thirty-two, it would be easy to assume that life circumstances are exclusively random.

The fourth-dimension perspective is that of the astral plane, or the energetic vibration just beyond our physical incarnate existence. In the astral existence, recently departed souls can pause before traveling into the spiritual realm to send an energetic communication to loved ones.

Many begin their spiritual awareness with an initial recognition of the nonlocal energetic world our human eyes do not see. Nonlocal consciousness arrives in our awareness through visual, emotional, and bodily sensation, and also cognitive awareness. Premonition, telepathy, and after-death communication are typical examples of energy transfer outside the third dimension.

When we first encounter these nongrounded, nonliteral information pathways, it is common to experience shock and disbelief. On the other hand, it is precisely such experiences of the nonlocal that lead many of us onto the seeker's path of higher consciousness and higher wisdom.

Operating with conscious awareness of your HS, you must gain a sense of trust that you may see your HS in your mind's eye. You may feel emotion as a signal that you are in communication with your HS, or you may feel a bodily sensation, such as your left eye twitching. You may feel pressure in your forehead from your HS, or you may receive literal thoughts coming from your HS. You may be blocked from finding a new job in your long-standing line of work, or you may keep reading about a particular spiritual program you are to attend as direct signs from your HS.

Our spiritual path will serve the highest good, and assist in heightening the vibration of our soul and that of the planet, only if we strive to experience the fifth dimension through our intuitive awareness.

As the earth continues to shift, allowing us greater access to higher vibrations and higher wisdom, we, as embodied souls, must assist ourselves in opening to more excellent knowledge and healing as individuals, both on this planet and within the universe. Our mission is to move forward into higher consciousness while incarnate in the third dimension—using the capable intuition we all have as a bridge to experience and gain awareness, knowledge, and behavior reflective of the ascended wisdom of the fifth dimension where our HS resides.

During soul regression, my clients recognize that they are benefiting from a higher level of consciousness and guidance. Concrete validation demonstrates that each past incarnation occurred with the intent to expand your evolution with purpose. We can know and experience, even kinesthetically, that we are each far more than this life, this body, or these current circumstances. This profound realization can lead to an altered view of life by highlighting that our life happenings are not meant to harm us but to educate us and allow us to inform others.

A past-life revelation and HS conversation bring us front and center with prebirth selections made for the upward climb of our soul and the evolution of humanity. Absorb the past-life account and the intricate prebirth plan of a middle-aged female soul regression client we will call Lisa. In her life today, she is in a same-sex partnership, works as a nurse, and copes with digestive issues.

LISA: Powerless as a Woman

My parents have decided I will marry a man they choose because he has money, and I am the oldest child. I'm in a wagon, all dressed up in a fancy dress. I'm taken to a party for him and me to announce our engagement. My mother tells me I am to be a good wife and care for him, but I don't want to get married. It feels like I live in Italy or Spain in a big house with beautiful gardens, and I don't want to leave here.

Once I am married, we have children, but I am not happy. I don't like it when he comes home. He's not gentle and often forces himself on me. Later, I am ill and old. My husband has died. My oldest son, whom I love very much, cares for me. I recognize him as my son of today. We have always been close.

I die and sense my soul flowing effortlessly out of my body. Several beings meet me and encourage me to come toward their light. They give me time to rest. I sense beautiful creatures like butterflies. Archangels Gabriel and Uriel are here and tell me I fear my own power.

I have had six earth lives and am not from earth. I have many guides who support me. One of them, whose name is Nallah, is like a lion. Nallah reminds me that we do not eat the meat of an animal where I come from; this is why I am a vegetarian in life today.

Also, I have a group of guides, like elderly women, called crones or queens. They care for me both in the spiritual realm and when I am in body on earth. They are maternal and mentor me to help my egoic mind quiet. My life purpose today is to take care of somebody else in need. Finally, they tell me I must remain incarnate on earth, though it is difficult here. The place I genuinely come from is peaceful, loving, and without gender. I must help raise the consciousness of earth.

• • • • • • •

Lisa's struggles in her current life are soothed by the perspective she gains during her soul regression when she connects to the soul-level awareness of her HS. In her regression, she learns of being forced to marry into an abusive situation. In life today, Lisa has made her own conscious relationship choice to be in a same-sex partnership. As humans, we live in a bifurcated culture where some folks are progressive about the nature of whom we love, while others, not so much. Digestive issues are common for IPS and ARS.

Relatedly, fear of our power is a recurrent issue for many. Lisa is met by two archangel guides, a strong indication that she is an experienced soul with an agreement to be of service on earth. Advanced guides, such as archangels, are assigned to support souls with more than a modicum of evolution. During my routine debriefing following a client session, Lisa acknowledged regression revelations that explain her life today. Her choice to work as a nurse mirrors the mentoring she receives from her feminine guides.

Ask Yourself

Do I fear my power? Said differently: Do I think small rather than big? Do I minimize my interests and capabilities?

Numerous elements explain why many of us frequently diminish ourselves in life today. First, our past lives often include events and relationships where parents mandated our lives, or our skills were minimized by the common belief of the time. Our soul energy is imprinted with the joys and sorrows of lives past. When our HS makes conscious the details of what occurred in prior incarnations, we know what is holding us back.

For some, being a soul who has reincarnated is a foreign concept. But as people on a spiritual journey, we need to embrace the truth of soul immortality and evolution. Our challenge is to function within a human culture, holding fast to our trust that we are souls having a human experience. Maintaining everyday communication with the wisdom that our HS has gained over time will support self-belief. With knowledge of all our lives and what our soul and human responsibilities entail, the HS places no value judgment on our soul evolution.

Prideful behavior is not in the nature of the fifth dimension. For our HS, it is expected and essential that we never boast about the evolution of our souls. Embodiment can be challenging as we expand our insight into who we are as a soul. Simultaneously, we must find a degree of comfort and functionality as humans. The challenge is to own our gifts and soul agreements in life today. People often question the truth of their gifts and undervalue themselves.

Also, remember that if we are an IPS and or ARS, we have not had most of our lives on earth. IPS and ARS know we are different from most folks on earth. Thus, it is easy to disempower ourselves with the notion that since we do not fit in anyway, why should we work hard to follow our soul agreements here on earth?

Lisa's regression reveals that she is not an EBS and lacks familiarity with earth life. With this knowledge, she locates the lost puzzle piece to clarify why she feels so different, experiences gastrointestinal tract discomfort, and much more. By not exclusively viewing life through a human intellectual perspective and honoring that she must nourish her mind, body, and spirit, Lisa empowers herself.

While earth life is dissimilar to Lisa's soul home of peace, love, and lack of gender bias, she is vigorously encouraged to stay the course of her life, and she knows that she has agreed upon intentions to aid humanity. Her cronelike guides are steadfast in their presence, as is her HS. She is now able to move forward in her life with a deep understanding of her prebirth preferences.

MICHAELA: Higher Self Wisdom Gathering

Michaela, a female client in her mid-forties, arrives for a between-lives soul regression, explaining that she feels lost about her future. She has left her governmental position and moved across the United States. She describes experiencing some degree of loss over that and uncertainty concerning her unsettled future. Michaela has been an elected state official capable of consequential responsibility. At the same time, she realizes she must leave a respected role to follow her heart, which tells her that a life change is in order.

A past life is discovered where she is discontented with her marriage and leaves the relationship. In her sixties, she finds peace and pleasure: there is a home surrounded by nature and a comfortable, loving relationship. Upon transcending into spirit, she is hugged by her familiar and positive spirit guide, Fandameer.

Through her regression, Michaela is shown with clarity that we must trust that when one relationship is unsatisfactory, a future relationship can bring pleasure and happiness. Leaving an unstable connection with someone is often required to bring forth a compatible bond with someone else. Also, our spirit guide is always right there at our side.

In her regression, Michaela is then taken to her soul group, the cohort of souls with whom she repeatedly incarnates. Her arrival unfolds in a joyful atmosphere with lots of exciting sharing. A discussion ensues about how mediocrity triggers boredom and discontent in her. Defining mediocrity is different for each of us.

Ask Yourself

How do I define mediocrity for myself? This is key because what one person defines as simply passable in life today can differ from someone else. For example, it may be your current-life agreement to live in your neighborhood, offering support to whoever is in need. For another person, the life intent may include running for elected office in a community, state, or country's legislative body. In her current life, Michaela found her role as a politician mediocre and lacking meaning. In collaboration with her HS, her guide Fandameer reveals that she is an experienced soul and must honor her need to aid others while taking time to be separate.

Fandameer reminds Michaela to lighten up and leads her to a private den where a door opens into the moonlight. Michaela is guided to meet with her council, her group of wise higher beings, who become unusually informal.

> *There are eight members in my panel of elders. Some are male, and some are female. The female members feel like a mom with lots of love. I feel a sense of recoil from this reunion with the elders. It is difficult to leave a life in the body and quickly cross into this sanctuary of contentment. This is a distinct place with a different feel from many of my past lives.*
>
> *The elders drop their formality. They are like friends of mine. They take off their robes and encourage me to take mine off too. The purpose of my current incarnation is to continue my research. The elders have compassion for my struggle in this current life. They tell me I have had the privilege of being in the human realm with all its earthly struggles.*

•••••••

Keywords stand out in Michaela's regression account: *sanctuary of contentment*, *take off their robes*, and *continue my research*. Our HS in the fifth dimension is responsible for aiding humanity, but it is not faced with the human trauma of romantic stress, monetary challenges, health issues, and so on. It is a sanctuary away from human events. A unique and telling signal in the regression is how the elders remove their robes, indicating they are on an even par with Michaela, who also removes her robe. Significantly evolved souls do incarnate to aid humanity, which is the case for Michaela. Her research is revealed in the following regression content, tied to life's surprises and disappointments.

> *I can recognize the divine nature of incarnate souls. I feel great love for these souls. I am in body to examine the beauty of the symphony of life, the surprises and disappointments. There are seeds I can plant to assist humans with their pain. My current life will not end for a while. I can serve as an instrument with others. I need much aloneness and separateness. It is hard to get close to people and their human energy. It is difficult to remain so separate. I must acknowledge and honor my sensitivity to the pain of human life.*
>
> *The elders are all in everyday street clothes. We are all sitting cross-legged on the floor. I am told that I, too, am a council member. I needed special permission to incarnate this time, and I may not incarnate again. I came to earth to understand human struggles from a deeper perspective and bring this information back to the spiritual realm. It is challenging to be in body and to acknowledge who I truly am, to access my divine nature without feeling that I am a freak. Others are council members embodied on earth. We are not superior. It is all about love.*

•••••••

Michaela speaks of several fundamental teachings, such as the need to have private time away from the energy of others. To grasp who we are as our HS is to leave ego aside. Our HS does not agonize about whether we can fulfill an agreement. Michaela agreed to embody on earth to experience the joys and trials at this time and to guide humans from the higher realm.

The words *to access my divine nature without feeling that I am a freak* speak loudly about knowing one is an experienced soul yet remaining humble. We *must* know and accept who we are as a soul and yet do what we came to do as humans. It is all about love and compassion for others.

Michaela is reminded of the privilege of—and the progress that can be made by—facing and coping with the ups and downs, the highs and lows, the joys and struggles that are possible only through incarnation as a human being. Each regression session is tailor-made by the spiritual realm to encourage conscious awareness of the living third-dimensional being and the advancement of the client's soul.

Ask Yourself

Even though I have struggled lately, what joy has happened simultaneously?

BONNIE: Guidance on Following One's Bliss

"Fear is created through a disconnect from the soul," stated Bonnie during her soul regression. She is a fifty-four-year-old client working in the corporate sector. Recently, Bonnie has discovered a new passion for incorporating stones into lovely jewelry of high energetic quality. Some would go as far as to call this work alchemy. One of Bonnie's critical questions during her regression was whether she should leave her corporate job and move exclusively into jewelry making.

Bonnie's answer continued.

The physical person needs to be supported in all ways possible for their success to achieve their soul contract. Few are awake, but many are coming awake. The planet earth and its inhabitants are slow to change. Those who can assist with change carry a higher density or vibration. You need to trust what you are drawn to do. Many become stuck in discomfort out of fear. For those who move out of fear, it is a true revelation to be who you truly are as a human and a soul. Unpredictability triggers fear. The trust of knowing and living your core nature is needed on the earth.

•••••••

Spirit supports Bonnie in following her heart and her passion. She was deeply encouraged during both regression sessions with me to trust her intuition and follow where she feels guided. In this way, she will allow her truth and her passion, stemming from divine awareness, to shine.

For many, by the end of the bird's-eye view that a soul regression provides into the depths of our core soul nature, everyday life is powerfully and significantly altered. Having the courage to heed that higher consciousness and transcend earthly material values provides unspoken rewards. While the individual soul benefits enormously from a regression experience, the earth and the universe reap a positive, literal, and energetic evolutionary change. When we live our human contract, we contribute to expanding our HS and the power of the higher realm.

Numerous scientists and authors continue to expound on the relationship between science and spirituality, examining the truth that our energetic selves can exist outside of form via quantum physics. We know emotion and intention guide our physical bodies, DNA, and life experiences. Many seek to consciously understand and explain the quantum space of uncontaminated divine force where our HS resides. Your HS is you at the soul level, who is ever present to bring forward signs in your everyday life about who you are and what you are meant to do.

One soul regression client discussed the neural net, or the nervous system of universal consciousness, during her session:

> *I would describe the neural net as the structure of consciousness (or the structure that consciousness creates), in which physicality connects itself into...the framework, or grid, if you will. It reaches through all creation, enlivens it, and brings spirit into matter. I believe that it is by connecting with this basic framework, like how the soul sings to the body at the time of ensoulment, that creation occurs. In learning to communicate with consciousness through the neural net, we begin to be able to move matter, manipulate matter, become multidimensional, and work with creation, space, and time. We connect with our soul, or HS, through this medium while we are ensouled.*

•••••••

So, you ask: How can I connect with the neural net or the energy grid that is the highway between our HS and everyday human life? The possibilities are endless for us to sense intelligence from our soul level. Intuition—whether imagery, emotion, body sensation, or thought—is one avenue. Tarot, numerology, automatic writing, drumming, essential oils, and crystals are only some ways to receive spiritual support and direction from your HS and guides. Trust is crucial to believe what you are receiving.

Take a moment now to appreciate a client whose guide is the highest member of the angelic realm. As you absorb these particulars, remember that we all have a guide, usually more than one. Carl's soul regression content begins with his past-life passing.

CARL: Michael's Guidance

I stay longer than I should at the scene of my death because of my husband in the past life. He did not deal with his grief over the death of our son. He closed his heart to me. Now, I feel the call or the pull as a soul to leave that life behind. I am home; it is good to be home. Home is light; there's an energy and a release. I feel like I am being recharged. It's so good to be home, but I am sad to leave my dear husband behind in that last life.

Now I feel a guide with me. It is Michael, the archangel. He tells me I am all here in spirit now, but I feel part of me has been left behind. This feeling of loss will be dealt with at a different time, not now. I will know when it is time to cope with the disconnect with the soul of my ex-husband of today, who was the husband in my past life. I remind Michael how happy we were in the privacy of our tepee when our son was small. That all went away when our son was gone.

I am told that when I was married (in my current life) to this same soul, we were to work out the pain of the past life. But, in life today, we did not do what we agreed. He's made mistakes. I did all I could, but I tried for too long. I am not to be so hard on myself. We have shared many lives and will have lives together again. In past lives, we shut each other out. In the future, we will have the chance to learn not to do this again.

•••••••

Carl's regression indicates three critical points. First, we experience being both male and female in past lives. Usually, we experience most of our lives as either a man or a woman, yet we must experience other perspectives to know how Mars is different than Venus. Second, Carl's soul has shared many lives with those of the past-life husband, suggesting they are from the same soul group. Michael cautions Carl not to be overly self-critical, as he's accomplished what was feasible in the past. Third, in a future embodiment, these two souls will retake the stage to figure out how to have an open heart with each other. Not all is lost, since a future chance is offered to step back into a relationship and find equilibrium with one another.

Once again, knowledge about our soul history and future-life plans from our HS sheds light on what has come before the current life, what was not resolved, and what can be healed in an upcoming incarnation. All is not lost, and we are not viewed as failing today.

In Summary

Regression hypnotherapy opens clients to the higher vibration of positive universal energy to achieve a mental understanding and spiritual awareness of their soul, their HS—the eternal affirmative nature of who and what they are. The process allows each client to swim consciously in the ocean of their soul within the greater universe while retaining memory of the experience after the regression is complete. Utilizing trance, the individual taps into personal and global DNA.

Emotions, physical health, and intuition are the language of our HS that reveals why we are embodied currently. Come to know and trust the signs of who you are as a soul and your life intentions, and you are situated to serve your soul agreements. What a gift it is to experience, through regression and intuition while in body, the awareness of who we are as a soul and the intentions of our present life.

We are each on our expedition as we traverse from body into spirit form and back again. And with every singular incarnation, we are learning, growing, developing, progressing, and advancing for the greater good of humanity. And we are not alone in our quest. The vast majority of between-lives soul regression accounts—in fact, the totality of cases I have personally gathered with my clients—attest that we have a full complement of spiritual guides, teachers, and companions. I invite you to meet some of them in the next chapters.

Things to Think About

- Your HS provides you with repetitive opportunities to stretch yourself, such as books, workshops, new work possibilities, new locations, and new people.
- Trust you can hear your HS, and you will.
- Consider your HS your best friend who calls you on your stuff and supports you unconditionally.

Homework to Strengthen Communication with Your Higher Self

1. Relax, breathe, and listen for the highest voice—*you*—who is not based on emotionality.
2. Pay attention to a sudden feeling of intense energy or anxiety. Ask your HS if new soul-level responsibilities have been added.
3. Consider skills and interests you have that do not show up in your life today, such as musical abilities but you are not a professional musician, or studying maps but you are not a cartographer.

CHAPTER THREE

Soul Design Evidence of Past Lives, Soul Origin, and Archetype

> I did not begin when I was born nor when I was conceived. I have been growing and developing through incalculable myriads of millenniums. All my previous selves have their voices, echoes, and promptings in me. Oh, incalculable times again shall I be born.
>
> —JACK LONDON

A deep dive into your soul's history and composition requires examining three vital factors. Initially, ponder this: It is nearly 100 percent certain that you have shared past lives with some of today's family members and friends. Past-life people, combined with easy and complex past-life occurrences, surface in your life now. Now consider that another ingredient of your soul are the unique skills, interests, and challenges based on whether your HS resides in the earthly spiritual realm (EBS), in the celestial realm (IPS), or in the energetic realm (ARS). Last, know that your soul carries a signature quality or archetype portrayed in each past life and today. All three ingredients demonstrate your immortal and intentional substance.

Soul Design: Past Lives, Soul Origin, and Soul Archetype

Each of us as a soul is complex with a unique tapestry. I aim to assist anyone interested in realizing their core nature or soul design. Think of your favorite recipe, with many components that lead to its intricate taste. All the sweet, spicy, tangy, and other flavors are analogies of the elements of who you are as a soul. Each of us is a blend of past-life experience, soul origination (earth, interplanetary, and angelic), and soul archetype (core characteristics). Your soul design is a weaving of embedded past-life content, your soul's origination, and the specific essence of seven possible energies.

Past Lives

To determine your ancestral bloodline, you can easily purchase a kit, swab the inside of your cheek, and access a window into your heritage. The discovery of your present life, family history, the timeline and location of your ancestors, who the community of your relatives is, and what health issues might be handed down becomes apparent. Soul regression allows us to mine a much more expansive picture of who we are as a soul across lifetimes.

Nearly fifty years ago, before I discovered regression, I began to study conventional psychology with two intentions. I am someone with endless curiosity about the why of everything. Why do we have certain attitudes, inclinations, fears, and skills? To evolve, we alter behavior that isn't useful for us and those around us. As I studied and ultimately opened my private psychology practice, I wanted to be able to answer various questions so that clients could comprehend themselves and make conscious decisions about current actions and choices.

My questions included: Did my mother's blind adoration of my brother, giving him no boundaries, explain the assumption he could abuse me at will? Am I strangely afraid of fire or flood because my parents expressed these fears? Do I worry that if I marry, it will end in divorce because my parents' marriage didn't last? Years ago, well before I understood the role of reincarnation, I wanted to help folks understand the origin of their thoughts and feelings. Also, I desired to assist people in finding ways to change their unwanted and intrusive attitudes.

An unexpected event happened in 1993 that dramatically altered my understanding of who we are as a soul. When my psychologist colleague passed, I began to intuitively sense his presence and scenes of past lives we had shared. Thirty years ago, I thought I had a grasp on what our nature, or this life's ancestry, and our nurture, or our current-life upbringing, mean as the distinct contributors to who we are as a person now. Humbly, I acknowledge that I was missing key elements of why we are the way we are.

Each of us is a composite of our genetic ancestral nature coupled with the specific contributions of our life circumstances as we advance from conception. Correspondingly, we are also souls with past-life experiences, soul origin—whether earth, interplanetary, or angelic—and the immortal archetypal quality of our soul.

Genetic Ancestral Nature and Soul History Must Be Examined

Ancestral healing applies to both your blood family and your soul family. The simple explanation is that in life today, some of your relatives are probably souls who have been key figures in your past lives. In the spiritual realm, we are never alone. Upon conception as a new soul, we join a small group of fellow souls, perhaps six to fifteen in number. These are the spiritual personalities with whom we are most closely affiliated—our soul cluster, or soul pod, as it were. At the soul level, known as our HS, we often collaborate and function with our fellow soul pod members.

Think of your bloodline and your soul line as overlapping. For instance, one of my grandchildren was my sibling in a past life. Events and the flavor of your previous relationship, often in more than one life, will color your current life with this soul/person. For instance, my sibling of the past may portray antagonistic behavior toward me in the present. Uncomfortable, dysfunctional behavior within a relationship today can be resolved by revealing what occurred in previous lifetimes. An element of our current-life blueprint often includes healing between ourselves and another soul where there has been trauma in a past life. Both people must be ready to do joint healing in today's life.

Soul regression is an irreplaceable tool to illuminate your past-life experiences. Grasping how past-life events explain your attachment to or discomfort with someone today will lead to the classic *aha* moment and a sense of calm. Little replaces the revelation of a prior link with someone that explains your current emotions. Please read about my client Nalanda, who discovers the bond with her son.

NALANDA: Inconsolable Loss and Regret Lead to Healing

I am in a past-life scene, walking with a young child. I have black lace-up leather shoes and a long, plain, black cotton dress. I wear a small hat with netting. My hair is pulled up, and I am an older governess.

The parents of this child have died. He is left to me to care for, but I am angry about this. I don't want to raise a child. Still, I love this boy, who is ten years old. I know what the right thing is to do, but I do the opposite anyway. I buy him a train ticket and send him to be with relatives out west. I don't believe that I can provide for him. He is so sad and cries. We hold hands against the window and the train leaves.

I find a note he left in my bag that says, "I love you." I harden my heart and walk away from the train station. I am very sad.

Now, it is twenty years later. I want to tell him why I sent him off and that I miss him terribly. I realize now that my son of today is the same soul as the boy who got on the train.

I am in bed now and am sick. I don't want to leave without seeing the boy who is a man now. My brother and niece are with me. I haven't seen the boy since he got on the train. We have had no contact. I just let go and die. Now I can see the boy I put on the train. He is thirty-two years old, with a wife and children. He is happy. Our hearts connect. It is okay now. Spiritual beings greet me. I feel loved and must release the sorrow from that life. These angels have come to meet me and remind me I am a caring and loving soul like them. They are playful, loving, and unburdened. They tell me that burdens are created by our mind; all we must do is shift how we see things. It is as simple as a thought.

In my work today, I help others with their pain. I am told that I had to feel inconsolable loss and regret to understand how to help others. As I help others clear their pain of loss, I clear my own and that of the planet.

I experience the pain of others so they do not have to carry so much pain; this is mercy and compassion.

I am told to go easy on myself and others. I am called to the path of healing. As I gain skills to help others release their pain, I must learn the energetics of not taking on their pain. I am honing my skills and will then teach them to others. My body moves easily and quickly; I can tolerate intense energy. This is good.

•••••••

Nalanda, a hospice counselor, works in the field of death and dying. Serving as the governess who was burdened by the loss of the boy for twenty years links the past with her current-life blueprint. The karma Nalanda may have incurred by sending the boy away is balanced by merging at the heart level with the boy's soul after her death. In this life, Nalanda also releases her guilt-pain karma by understanding, supporting, and energetically aiding the dying and their families in their grief.

Nalanda's son of today, Bradley, is the boy of the past and is a member of Nalanda's immediate soul family. The providence of her blueprint appears, indicating the purpose for Nalanda and Bradley's strong bond as mother and son. Our relationships of today open a portal to mend the past.

Conventional psychology leads most of us to think about life today with numerous questions beginning with the word *why*. For instance: "Why am I afraid to travel more than two hours by car from home? Was my mother or father afraid of traveling any distance from home?" Another example would be: "Why do I suffer from unexplained back pain? Did my mother or father have chronic back pain?" Problems with leaving home and back pain suggest the possibility that we may have a learned behavior or a genetic propensity for physiological symptoms. A more complex discernment can arise with the question: "Does my ability to receive intuitive input from my guides, as I detach to channel, arise from my current life having to cope with childhood abuse? Or did I gain the skill to convey soul-level guidance during one or more past lives?" Once again, soul regression clarifies our past lives, soul origin, and soul archetypal nature.

Ask Yourself

Is there someone in your life (or who has been in your life but has passed) with whom your relationship is acutely, perhaps unexplainably, meaningful? Or, the reverse, is there a person whom you are constantly triggered by and don't want to be around? In both cases, it is almost a sure thing that you've shared numerous lives. Add to the mix what you fear that seems illogical. Past-life details can surface in soul regression, and you can also determine past incarnations through self-examination.

Soul Origin: Earth Based, Interplanetary, or Angelic Realm

As humans, we are more complex than many would assume. Think of yourself like a cooking recipe with a complex sweet, salty, and spicy flavor profile. Your past lives play a role in your loves and love-nots as a third of the recipe defining you. The original formation of your soul explains another third of the energy of your current self. In the vast celestial realm, souls are created to embody on earth (EBS) primarily. Plus, there are souls intended to function somewhere in the universe that could be a planet, star, and the like (IPS). Finally, as discussed, a third origination of souls is in the angelic realm that serves the higher or divine force (ARS).

The following account of a soul regression experience provides a potent example of an IPS and the purpose of solitude in life. To deepen your understanding, absorb this extensive soul regression transcript for Chase, a man in his fifties, along with his observations in the weeks and months following the session.

CHASE: Different Strokes

During the interview, Chase volunteers the following information about his life: "Most people, it seems, have a drive to get married and have children. I never had that drive, though I am very attracted to women. In recent years, I have thought it would be rewarding to have children. On the other hand, I have observed the downsides of being married and having children. One doesn't have the freedom of being single. I've always appreciated being independent and even alone. I don't feel that I need someone's company to enjoy myself. When I'm home alone, I don't pine for companionship. I don't feel lonely."

It's day, and I am flying a biplane I'm testing. I have on goggles and a brown leather helmet. There's a problem, and the engine stops. I pull the levers but can't get the engine started. The plane sputters and keeps going down. I am scared. The plane crashes.

My soul left before the plane crashed. I designed the plane and am disappointed. I want to tell someone that it's okay that I have died. Spirit tells me that I did fine. My brother fixed the mechanical problem after the crash. He fixed something under the steering choke stick. My brother and I worked on this repair together because he received my intuitive direction about what to fix.

Gary, a lifelong friend, meets me as I expand into the spiritual realm. We're laughing hysterically. Here we are again. Gary and I have shared a lot. We've known each other for more than one life.

• • • • • • •

Chase describes his past life, having died in a plane crash. As you take in Chase's completely spontaneous regression content, you meet Gary. You encounter Gary's HS, whom Chase meets in the higher realm because Gary is alive. Gary is part of Chase's soul ancestry, though they are not blood relatives in life now.

We pass some structures made of light. This area is essential and sacred. There are books along the side. There are people there doing research. They are doing the same research as I am. They are looking at their books. There is a dark blue sky or space inside the books. There is a green-looking guy here who helps people with their research. Some souls need help finding their books. The books are like energy packets.

"You're not from around here originally. It might take a while to get used to it...being on earth, that is." The green guy points to a glowing area

that opened in the book. "That's where you are from. You incarnated on earth three hundred years ago and have had seven lives there." The green guy is tall with delicate features. It is easier where I am from; people are gentler and more spacious. People do not get in each other's way. I was more advanced on that planet.

• • • • • • •

I notice immediate clues as I sit alongside clients and listen to their regressions. When structures of light are mentioned, I know that my client has traveled to a high frequency. Research in the higher realm is ongoing to aid the earth's and the universe's expansion. A green guy, a guide, tells me that my client is an IPS who does not originate in earth's frequency. The home base for an IPS is always a healthy culture, described as being gentle and advanced.

I am told that my human body has a nervous system problem because of the adjustment to being on earth. My sleep, chest, and alcohol issues are tied to not being here on earth for very long. I do not need to force the adjustment. I should not smoke cigarettes. It makes me more nervous. The green guy turns up the volume from the planet where I am from so that I can feel my home more.

I am on the edge of more extraordinary things. My life purpose is to evolve in consciousness. It is not about a mate or things. It is about more excellent vision. I must raise my consciousness even more. Even when I drink, I can still develop greater consciousness. I am working with more profound levels of confusion to gain clarity.

I am bathed in green light for greater comfort and energy. This helps my liver. It is suggested that I try more art. My life on earth has broken through more spiritually. It is happening quicker than I think.

• • • • • • •

Unfortunately, IPS often must cope with physical challenges because they lack experience in the human body. Of crucial importance is that as IPS, we always agree to incarnate; we are never coerced. All the same, some of our incarnations are significantly challenged physically, emotionally, and spiritually. Caring for our health is essential. Chase learns it is not necessary to have a mate in life today. Holding fast to the understanding that confusion leads to clarity and greater consciousness is remarkable for him.

For each of us as a soul and in each life, the degree of solitude from which we will benefit varies. Chase's soul regression is a clear example of a life where solitude is preferred. He learns that relative isolation in this lifetime will allow him the opportunity to dive deep into spiritual awareness.

Chase is also an example of a soul whose HS exists somewhere in the celestial realm that is not earth. Consequently, Chase is an IPS soul with unique qualities and skills. Terms synonymous with IPS are *star seed* or *extraterrestrial*. Often, an individual with such broad-based dimensional experience will face literal physical/medical issues, as their soul is more familiar with a different container, if you will.

After his soul regression, Chase shared the following insight: "I think my guide gave me that infusion of energy because he's a healer. He knew what I could take. He plunged me into a health crisis that compelled me to stop drinking. I haven't had a drink or smoke since I don't know when. I may have quit entirely."

Chase provides a powerful bird's-eye view into the benefits and liabilities of using chemical substances to enter an altered state. As many of you know, there are healthier means to connect at a deeper intuitive level, such as meditation, shamanic journeywork, and other options.

Listening weekly to regression clients for many years, I have never heard a word spoken suggesting the divine shakes a fist or finger at any of us; quite the contrary. Repeatedly, I hear a loving appeal from the teachers in spirit for clients to let go of creating more suffering in life. Instead, they would have us view each occurrence as a means of progression, an event drawing us toward a new and expanded perspective. Why waste our lives blaming ourselves for many things we should or should not have done?

Soul design has a final component. Thus far, we've pieced together that your past lives contribute to your relationships, skills, avoidances, health issues, worries, historical and geographical interests, and much more. The second and equal element to your soul design, your uniqueness, is related to whether you were created to primarily come to earth or function most of the time in the vast celestial or angelic realm.

Nalanda teaches us that a soul as important as the past-life boy, who was not her son, can opt to be her beloved present-life son. Our past directly explains our present. Your soul design expands as you learn whether the origination of your core self is to sequence lives on earth, or in an extraterrestrial location, or at the frequency level of the angel souls who embody pure love energy. Think of soul design as a formula, like DNA, that explains who you are as a soul and in life today.

Ask Yourself

Did you grow up fascinated with the night sky and always wish to be out there somewhere? You are likely an IPS. Did you grow up with a sense of divine energy even if you did not find organized religion appealing? You are likely an ARS. Do you feel you're more adapted to the ills of humans than other spiritual people you know? You are likely an EBS.

Soul Archetype: One through Seven

Your soul has a flavor—distinct, ageless, and fixed. As a baby soul on the brink of your first incarnation, the selection of a soul archetype is set in stone and assigned by your spiritual guides. A myriad of factors leads to your soul signature and your soul nature. First, the seven energies must be balanced in the higher realm and on earth. Of these seven options, only one flavor is the backbone of your soul, as your HS and throughout your incarnations.

Grasping your soul archetype or soul ray will undoubtedly provide insight into who you are today and in all your lifetimes. Your soul and human characteristics will be illuminated as you discern which of the seven energies is yours for eternity. To grasp your archetype, consider your most vigorous skills and passion. Archetype one is the change agent energy that guides the higher realm and earth forward. United States supreme court justice Ruth Bader Ginsburg is a prime example. Nonetheless, your coworker or next-door neighbor can also be archetype one. The one archetype is strong, directive, and unafraid of new ideas. Two of my previous books further explain the seven archetypes (*The Evolving Soul* and *Souls on Earth*).

Archetype two catalyzes the intense force of cognitive ideas and energy of renewal into cultural acceptance founded in love and compassion. Pope Francis carries the soul energy of two as he demonstrates that all people's needs must be met. An initial upright triangle of coordinated energy is formed by archetype one at the apex, with two and three as the base of support for one. The one force leads off the energy of shift and is supported by two's love. Archetype three is the crucial third leg of the stool, as the soul and person who melds knowledge and wisdom to serve humanity's evolution in small and, at times, more obvious ways. As a professional psychologist/regression therapist, wife, mother, grandmother, friend, and more, I've always enjoyed expanding my knowledge and spiritual awareness. Thus, I am a three.

We turn to archetype four, equally crucial energy in the higher realm and on earth. Think of artistry or the balance of aesthetic elements, and you have four energy. Musicians, actors, artists, chefs, and others hold the essential energy of creative elements. Beethoven and da Vinci are four souls. Archetype five is also a balancing agent, but it differs from four. Four relates to creative balance more from a feeling, and esoteric standpoint. Five is grounded in structure, logistics, and a concrete plan to provide stability. My husband, Earl, is an administrator extraordinaire and is archetype five. An additional example of a five is President Joe Biden.

Archetype six is truly a powerhouse whose energy is focused on the cohesion of group energy, such as a family, ethnicity, or country. Six archetypes are zealous about the need to function in community. World-renowned tenor Andrea Bocelli and President Barack Obama are examples of six souls. To bring the archetypal energy of one through six into an alchemy and sustainability, we arrive at archetype seven. Souls and people who maintain the seven energy are strongly humanitarian in expanding our human world. Sevens are also crucial at the HS level to merge and balance the orientation of souls one through six into a transformation composite.

Francis Bacon and Frank Lloyd Wright are examples of souls as humans who are the force of seven.

The seven archetypal energies manifest a divine composite of behavior, thought, and action coupled with caring, compassion, and love to transform humanity in alignment with the higher realm. Soul regression, both into past lives and to a conscious bond with my client's HS, reveals the soul archetype, which honors our skills, abilities, and intentions. Absorb Jeanne's soul regression, which shows her initially painful discovery of her strength to stand firmly committed to not marrying someone she does not love. In the end, you'll notice that happiness and soul transformation prevail. Jeanne's soul archetype will become evident as you contemplate her regression material and my commentary.

JEANNE: Facing Hardship for the Good of All

I'm outside alone in an open meadow where the temperature is comfortable. I have coarse leather shoes. I have a skirt and a shawl that are not fancy, more like work clothes. My skin is white, and I have long brown hair pulled back in a single braid. As an older teenage girl, I feel torn about loving the scene and being afraid of loss.

I've been in this place all my life, and it is peaceful and beautiful. Yet I'm afraid I will have to leave. I've been married off and do not want to go. I am afraid and couldn't have a say about my to-be husband. I don't like him. He's an older farmer, and I will just be worked and used. There's no kindness or joy. My life as I have loved it is over. I am very, very sad. I see no way out.

•••••••

More often than I can count, I've had clients (almost always women in life today) who discover a past life where their parents arranged a forced marriage. I assume that the higher realm not only wants the client to release the trauma of fear about stepping into an unwanted marriage but also the historical trauma of the unhealthy control of women. I am sure you have noted that Jeanne's past life's intense despair is triggered by her feeling powerless.

The upcoming detail of Jeanne's past life will pull at your heartstrings. To avoid further interruption in your reading of this intense past life, let me note here that an attempt to take one's own life likely has been a factor, at least once, for many of us in our past lives. I invite you to trust that there is a distinct purpose for Jeanne to know about this prior embodiment.

I wonder if I could drown myself. I feel despair. I look at the pond, but I don't know if I can do it. But I want to do it. I can't bear the thought of what is in store for me. He's cruel.

I move to the edge of the pond. Then I see some rocks. I can put them in my pocket. I load my pockets. I walk farther in, but my shoes are sticking in the muck. Now the water is up to my shoulders.

My heart is just breaking because I love to be alive. My mother will feel so sad. I don't know if I can do it. I hear her call me. Then I see her running to me and calling and calling.

She gets to the edge of the pond. She begs me to come out and says she won't be able to stand it if I do what I was intending. Mom says that if I don't come out of the pond, then she will come in. (Client is crying hard.) If I do this, she will do it too.

I don't know what to do. I look at my mother, and we are both sobbing. Neither of us knows what to do. A dog comes and barks, making so much noise that someone else comes. It is my father. There's shouting and anger. He says, "What are you doing? Come out of there right now. You will shame me. I will have to leave."

He keeps telling us to come out. There's concern, fear, anger, and blame. My brother comes now and pleads for us to come out. "We need you."

Now my younger sister comes crying. We move back out of the water. My sister is distraught and holds on to both of us as she cries. My brother is both angry and crying. He asks, "Why would you do this?" My mother and I are dripping wet, and someone brings a blanket.

We walk back to the house across the field. My father is at a loss. He had no idea how desperate I felt. He threatens to beat us. He goes back and forth between being angry and devastated. My father tells me I can't be trusted. He makes me spend the night in the barn until I come to my senses because going into the pond is behaving like a farm animal. He says I am bringing shame to my family.

I am overwhelmed because it's too intense and has so much emotion. I don't want to hurt my family, but I can't go toward what they have arranged. I feel so desperate. So I start to think I could throw myself out of the upper part of the barn. Some part of me will not do what feels so unbearable to imagine. He will not stop me. I will find a way. I could set fire to the straw in the barn.

It is later now. I am in a farmhouse. I have a lovely little girl at my knee. I'm not married to the cruel old farmer. I am married to somebody who loves me. I'm happy. I'm singing and making bread. I think the old farmer died unexpectedly. That plan was aborted. This man that I love sought me out. We are so happy together. I'm pregnant now. This was around the time of the 1600s. I know a lot about herbs.

Now it is the very last day of my life. My daughter is with me and my grandchildren. I'm on my deathbed. People have come to say goodbye. I have been loved and respected. My husband is there holding my hand. I drift off to sleep as I move toward dying. I feel peaceful and know that I will be missed. Dying is easy, and I am relieved.

I feel great tenderness as I look at the woman I was. I know the hardships she survived. The struggle is over. I am proud of her. There is grief about leaving my family, wanting to tell them that I will linger and help as much as I can. My past-life husband is the soul of my current spouse.

•••••••

Jeanne's overwhelming past life portrays the depth of her fortresslike resistance to marrying a man she does not love. Notice this family's nearly impenetrable collective energy committed to their mutual bond. Even the father intends to honor his integrity and agreement with the neighbor farmer. Jeanne's soul regression demonstrates a family energy of solidarity called soul archetype six.

Archetypes two, four, and six are people whose core way of being is right-brained or based on emotions and caring. Six is fiercer than two and four, with a keen direction that humans must function within groups with loyalty beyond measure. As archetype six, Jeanne demonstrates her zealous attitude in following what she believes is right. She stands her ground but remains within her family until she wins out over her father and finds true love.

Now I feel like I am coming home. I feel happy now where there is purple and green energy. I feel warmly welcomed back. My guides are here. They are proud of me for how courageously I lived and the kindness I expressed.

I am taken to a playground where I swing, and they laugh with me. Together, we dance and play. It is like a party. Next, they bring me to a hammock and invite me to climb in and rest. In my life today I am to play more. My guides tell me I should stay there longer. They know I need some time off. I'm told they want me to lighten up, giving me plenty of time to not worry about what I need to know in this location.

We go to a garden and sit by the fountain. It is time for them to answer the questions I brought to this soul regression. There's plenty of time to figure out things in this life. Even if I don't latch on to everything, I want to comprehend this all-right life. I should play more and be brave less.

I cannot fix my husband's outbursts. Walk away as needed. I'm to relax more. Also, I need to take my power back with my brother. My guides are pretty silly. They tell me they like to tease me to suggest that I become more playful without so much seriousness. I'm to release my fear.

As I ask my guides about the vertigo I experience, and they tell me it is about rebalancing the relationship with my spouse. I'm to stop bracing myself in case he has an outburst. They tell me to move into my own choices and entitlement. My guidance team firmly asks me to stop carrying people on my shoulders, which causes bracing and vertigo. As I let go of the need to rescue, my body will stop holding so much tension.

My guides tell me I am an EBS. I sense they are holding me as if in a cradle. I can feel their comfort and protection. They tell me that all will be well.

• • • • • • •

Most humans, especially experienced souls, need more time for play. I invite you to take to heart the picture Jeanne's guides have painted, which states that resting in a hammock is prescribed. Jeanne's guides' advice is plentiful as she is invited, even implored, to take care of her own needs and not tense her body in fear that her husband will lack control in his responses. The only control we have is of ourselves and no one else. As Jeanne said, providing ongoing support is the apparent role of our guides. Archetype six people are always committed to the cause of the collective, whether family, work group, community, or more.

Ask Yourself

Do you know the details of at least three or four of your past lives, and is there a common thread that signifies your soul archetype? If not, think about activities and commitments you're most passionate about, and there, you will find your soul archetype.

Soul Design: A Creative Tapestry

Complex, intricate, and intentional words describe our unique soul design. Think of your design as an overlay of three essential components. A house must have a foundation that is secure and stable. Such is the case for your soul. Your soul origin, whether EBS, IPS, or ARS, is the specific, grounded component of your soul's conception. A higher frequency of wisdom determines your soul origin. If you are an IPS, your soul has unique qualities tied to your home location in the expansive celestial realm. As an EBS, you were created to evolve over innumerable earth lives to expand and learn. When you are an ARS, and you agree to an earth embodiment, your task is to exude pure caring energy and action among humans, animals, and all living things. The birthplace of your soul is the genesis of your makeup.

With your soul origin foundation in place, the next step to build *you* of today is your soul archetype, meaning the nature or personality of your core. As an EBS, your archetype is determined upon conception of your soul. All ARS are soul archetype two, to carry compassion as their passion during incarnation on earth. Because the archetypal structure of seven options defines the overall intent of humanity to evolve, an IPS is designated with their archetype when they initially agree to an earth incarnation. Your soul archetype is precisely who you are meant to be as you approach daily life. Each of the seven archetypal energies is perfect and beneficial. The additive sum of all seven energies is essential to evolve earth's higher realm and life.

No less important is the final third of your soul design. Each past life is imprinted on your soul energy with the most prominent details of your trials and accomplishments. As an EBS, almost all your incarnations have happened on earth. Upon reaching an experienced evolutionary level, an EBS has waded or sailed through hundreds, if not thousands, of lives.

Both an IPS and an ARS may have few past lives at all. When an ARS incarnates, their embodiment happens on earth, explained by the core of their energy that is tied to the high-frequency guidance of earth's Source. God has many labels, such as Source, Great Spirit, the Manu, and others. Last, an IPS may or may not have past lives. IPS clients range from having had fewer than five earth lives to as many as a hundred earth lives. An IPS may or may not have had past lives somewhere in the celestial realm.

I invite you to stay tuned to the upcoming chapters illuminating the unique qualities and potential past lives of all three soul origin types. Remember that your soul design and others are multifaceted works of art.

In Summary

Nalanda teaches all of us that loss is inevitable. How we cope with it, whether in past lives or today, can help us deepen our understanding of loving, losing, and regaining. She feels a heartwarming relief as she discovers that the young boy found love and peace in his adult life. Even more crucial for Nalanda is the inexplicable beauty of having her son of today be the soul of the past-life boy. Past lives are inextricably embedded in our soul's journey, revealing how the trauma of past embodiment can be released.

Melding the elements of soul design, we come to Chase's discovery that he is not a soul designed to incarnate on earth. The understanding arises that for some, living a more solitary life is healthy and intended to hold the energy of higher consciousness for humanity's expansion. As an IPS, Chase realizes that his human body is reactive due to his only having a few earth lives. Your soul tapestry is another crucial component of your soul archetype. Jeanne teaches us about perseverance that maintains the stability of a pack or a cooperative guild. As Jeanne's family pleads with her to remain steadfast, she finds the ability to stand firm in her family while not sacrificing her ultimate happiness with a life partner. Consider the impetuous but resilient strength of Jeanne's soul archetype six behavior.

Now you have it: The compound structure of your soul as soul origin, soul archetype, and past lives. I invite you to strive to know yourself at the level of your soul design. Your soul essence today is a blending of soul design elements and your life's intentions, also labeled life purpose.

Things to Think About

- Your ancestral bloodline overlaps your past-life history, meaning your child of today could have been a particular person in your past life.
- An EBS adapts more easily to human life than an IPS or ARS and experiences physical, emotional, and spiritual challenges to adapt on earth.
- Soul archetype is immortal and revealed in your qualities and commitments in each past life.

Homework to Determine Your Soul Design

1. What country, time in history, or extraterrestrial environment have you always wanted to visit that could be a clue to your past lives? Have you always felt that you didn't come from earth?

2. Is your orientation to life as archetype two that all people's needs must be satisfied? Or do you want to study and learn continuously as archetype three?
3. Consider your passions in life, such as teaching children, painting, or scientific research. Our life intentions are revealed in how we love to spend time in life today.

CHAPTER FOUR

Earth-Based Soul Essence in Past Lives, Higher Self, and Today

> Good for the body is the work of the body, good for the soul the work of the soul, and good for either the work of the other.
>
> —HENRY DAVID THOREAU

Embodied souls on earth come in three categories. I like to explain this triad of unique souls with the word *origin*. Your soul originates from a location in the celestial realm. Is the genesis of your soul, and the intended locale of your HS, tied to the energy of earth, the vast universe outside of earth's frequency, or the angelic realm that serves humanity? Ninety to ninety-five percent of all humanity consists of EBS. Most of these incarnated EBS are moderately evolved, meaning they've gained a midrange level of soul development. Stay tuned for chapters 5 and 6, which focus on souls from the greater celestial realm (IPS) and souls from the angelic realm (ARS).

Who Are You as an Individual Evolving Soul?

If you are an EBS, you come into the body to progress as a soul. Initially, your soul is spun out of the Tao, or born as a spark of the primordial essence of the universe. This divine energy has been given many names, such as Great Spirit, Tao, God, Source, Elohim, and Christ consciousness. No matter what term you prefer, your soul stems from this highest vibrational energy of wisdom and truth that seeks to guide humanity. Strong nurturance and intense schooling from within the spiritual realm are essential before your very first incarnation so that you can adjust to life on earth.

Just as a child needs to develop social and educational abilities, you, as an EBS, have an innate impetus to reach higher levels of spiritual learning. Advanced souls residing in the celestial realm are your classroom teachers as you begin the equivalent of preschool-level training to prepare your soul for incarnation. Think about the critical job of a parent who initially cares for every need of the newborn and toddler, then expands to school-based knowledge.

After your newborn and toddler education in the celestial realm, you are sufficiently prepared as a soul to begin the earth school of evolution from one lifetime to the next. At approximately age five, a child is ready to take that first step toward independence by beginning school, away from their parents. This is like your birth into physical embodiment and the subsequent steps through life on earth, which provides the dense and challenging laboratory of learning you need to reach expanded degrees of soul evolution.

The elements of incarnational learning are relationships, health, loss, and a few other common areas. Take a moment to think about and examine their impact on your life. What experiences have challenged you, yet been the most effective teaching tools? Embrace the seemingly problematic issues in your life as divinely inspired opportunities to broaden and expand your learning. How you deal with the not-so-easy circumstances in life often correlates with the number of rungs you climb up that proverbial ladder of soul development and the speed with which you do it.

You incarnate as an EBS to advance both your own wisdom and collective wisdom. Moving through your lifetimes from denser to more excellent light, you advance from incarnations centered on your soul's progress to lives serving humanity's progress. The knowledge that you achieve through each lifetime not only benefits you as an individual soul, but your trials and tribulations also enhance the greater whole of humanity and the universe. Your intrinsic reason for incarnating gradually becomes more accessible and easier to discern. You discover that you are here to be of service. Eventually, you reach a level of development where you serve as a teacher or guide for other souls. Some advanced souls opt to continue incarnating on earth to progress their learning and that of others.

You are where you are on the path, be it the equivalent of grade two, grade twelve, or graduate school. Life on earth presents the challenges you must face to acquire the ability to operate in human life from the vantage point of your soul versus your human-egoic self. It is the crucible where you learn to overcome the soul-deadening grip of human fear and worry and to trust that you are always loved and supported by the higher realm. Whether simple or complex, each ingredient of your life is a prospect for progress.

So, no matter your life choices, all is well because you are repeatedly given another opportunity to learn. Each life event is a course in your earthly classroom set in motion by the soul agreements you've put in place. Your awareness of why you are here now will expand when you accept that what needs to happen simply happens. Or, to put it in a slightly different way, when you acknowledge that the events and people in your life are put in place to enhance the evolution of your soul and that of others, then you know such life lessons stem from the wisdom of your soul and your guides' prodding.

Every lifetime has a soul-designed curriculum for enhancing and expanding your soul awareness and capability. When you accept that all experiences in life serve the purpose of moving you to a higher grade in the school of soul development, life becomes manageable. All the events in your life offer a window into who you are, why you are here, and how you can continue advancing as a soul. Benevolent spiritual guidance is always available to support you on your onward journey. My best advice is to trust, and to accept fear as a signal that you are facing an opportunity to grow.

Even after thirty years of guiding soul regression, the power and insight gained by my clients via their intuitive regression revelations continue to impress me. My understanding of the soul expands with each person I lead. Frequently, my clients might minimize their learning in a past life until their guides clarify the value of perseverance through loss. Join me as you travel with Amalia, as an EBS, through her in-depth between-lives soul regression. Imagine you are observing the upcoming regression through a one-way mirror as I share explanations and commentary with you in writing.

AMALIA: Soul Expansion through Past-Life Love and Loss

I'm a middle-aged woman living during colonial times in the United States, and war is going on. I'm outside in the countryside, and it's hot. I have an everyday dress that is modest and has a high neck. My hair is blonde under a bonnet. Men have been fighting, and many are wounded. I'm not a nurse. I feel numb and empty as I watch the men who have survived.

I'm walking toward the village, and the soldiers are behind me. No one is talking to each other. There's a sense of shock. This is my village, and I can't find my husband. Suddenly, I'm so sad and empty. I realize that my husband died in the battle. I'm on the main street of my village and feel dumbfounded. I just fall to my knees crying.

Rather quickly, I stand up and swallow my feelings. I want to wail more, but I stand up and keep walking blindly. It's been months since he passed, and I'm terribly lonely. Years go by, and the death of my husband still bothers me.

It's later now. I'm in a surgeon's office on my stomach. I have a bullet in my back, and he's trying to get it out. There's lots of blood. There's nothing more in my life for me to stay. I'm in my late forties. I've died now and am glad I let go. It was definitely time to move on. I see the table with my body on it.

For a few moments after dying, I feel fear in my chest. Soon thereafter, the fear is completely gone. I'm in bright energy with comfort and familiarity. There's nothing scary. I'm so happy.

•••••••

Trauma hones us as we determine how to cope with death. For that matter, know that loss of any sort, whether physical or emotional, has the intent and potential to influence our soul evolution. We are to keep putting one foot in front of the other and find a way to continue our lives steadfastly. Take a few moments and write down two or three loss events in your life that have been transformational.

I sense a comfortable golden energy on my right side that has no form. I know this is one of my guides, Gold. My guide has feminine energy and feels soft. My guide tells me, "Job well done. Your art of living was well done with integrity and compassion. It is not essential to identify the soul of the past-life husband."

Now my guide takes me to a gateway with other entities and energy bubbles. This is a bright arrival point. I'm in a space that has a concrete look with a stone floor and a window. Gold is still with me.

I come to a table with eight energies or souls around it. There is a place for me at the table, and Gold is behind me. My guide encourages me to step up to the table. I am intimidated by being at the table with these essential energies. It is time for me to report to them, and they will process my testimony.

They ask what I learned. I tell them about the importance of human connection and love. It was through the loss that I learned this. They affirm my learning. Through the depths of my love for my husband, I gained a great deal. They tell me that it is irrelevant to know who the soul of my husband was.

They agree with my learning assessment, and I feel their support. Their acceptance of me and learning about human love is essential. Is that the only thing I am supposed to get from this past life? They tell me that stuffing my emotions is something I need to work on. I don't feel insulted by their comment. I feel that is what they wanted to say. I am dismissed.

• • • • • • •

We always have at least one guide in the higher realm supporting our life intentions and soul progress. Chapter 7 details the unique distinctions of guides among EBS, IPS, and ARS. Amalia's guide, Gold, is likely a highly experienced soul, as evidenced by the name Gold indicating a high-frequency color. Guide qualities, such as feminine and soft, suggest Amalia focus on her tender, graceful approach to life. Gold pats Amalia on the back for her past lifestyle of maintaining integrity and caring.

As we walk through Amalia's between-lives soul regression, characteristics of an EBS are on display. Facing and accepting the human loss experience is one of the numerous required embodied challenges we must surmount. Our guides do not desire denial of our emotional pain related to loss. The motto to adopt is to feel the pain and keep living day by day. I often say that emotional pain while incarnate is the sandpaper of soul evolution.

Amalia's guide delivers her to the gateway arrival point. During between-lives soul regression, the client transitions from the memory of a past life on earth in the third dimension through the portal into the fourth dimension, or astral plane, and connection with her HS. Our HS is accessible when we learn to trust our intuition.

Upon completion of every past life, we must meet with a group of advanced souls who insist we are candid about what we conclude were our past life accomplishments and inadequacies. If we are honest, our interrogative panel will be satisfied. Human connection and love are crucial elements for maturation as an EBS. The challenging loss of Amalia's husband in the past life, notwithstanding her soul evolution, is what launches her realization of the value of deep love and commitment. For some clients, it is crucial to uncover the current-life identity of a soul from past life. It is likely unimportant for Amalia because she does not know the soul of her past life in today's incarnation.

Finally, Amalia is strongly advised not to deny her emotions in her current life. By honoring her deep love for her husband and her grief in her past life, Amalia's guides indicate the expansive power of her being honest with herself. The session is concluded when these primary teachers determine they have accomplished what was needed.

Now I want to go someplace that is peaceful and alone. I am back with my guide, Gold. I go to a place like a library with stone walls and oversized windows. It looks out over a beautiful garden with grass and trees. I am here to empty and let go with a sense of neutralizing. I need some quiet time here for a bit.

I'm told it is time to see my friends. Gold guides me into a white-light space. I'm with my group now. There is no form, but I see ten, or maybe twelve, energy bubbles that are joyful I'm back with them. All of us are the same size of energy that is translucent with silver or gold on the outside.

The energy bubble to my left wishes to welcome me back with celebratory energy. The soul to my left is a companion in many of my lives. This bunch of souls is not very serious right now and wants a relaxing party.

Most of my lives happen on earth. Some of this group of about twelve souls usually incarnate with me. The soul to my left is with me in most lives and usually takes the primary teacher role to instigate the most learning. The others are supporting actors.

•••••••

My clients often need quiet, neutralizing time during their HS visit in the regression. Appealing descriptions of the place of rest are common. Though the earthly spiritual realm has no density, I am sure there are locations of rejuvenation that lend themselves to human qualities of water, sound, and vibrant colors. I do not doubt that our guides know when we require renewal, tied to the complexity of our past life and/or our life today.

Next on Amalia's agenda is to meet with her neighborhood group of souls, with whom she incarnates most often and who support another's soul evolution. EBS always belong to a small soul pod of ten to twenty souls created simultaneously. The client feels welcome relief when they consciously reencounter their friends. These souls would include some of your family members, close friends, key mentors, neighbors, coworkers, and the like.

My group is waiting for me to do something. They want me to tell my story of the past life I just discovered. I am sharing what I learned about love and its importance. The group learns from me as I learn from the one to my left. Now my group takes time to socialize.

I go with the one to my left to the library where I was earlier. My energy joins with this other soul. This helps me shake off the remnants of the past life I just left. The two of us are very connected and don't need to talk. We've been together for a very long time. The one to the left helps me ground. Being with this one helps me become whole again.

Life in the body is hard work. Life has expectations, responsibilities, and playing a character. We evolve primarily in body, not out of body.

•••••••

Amalia demonstrates how her soul pod benefits from the enlightenment an earth life can provide. A romantic love relationship of equality and devotion is a rung on the ladder of soul evolution for an EBS. One soul pod member in immediate proximity to Amalia is central to supplementing the knowledge she gains. Within an EBS pod, generally, there are two or three other souls who collaborate with your soul evolution. It is noteworthy how much time Amalia's group takes for pleasure, which is another common camaraderie component. Think about who you feel is a critical person in your life to inflate your growth and enjoyment.

The soul to the left takes charge in helping Amalia release traumatic energy from their past life. All EBS have a soul or two with whom they've shared the most lives. Plus, one other soul pod member was created to be the supportive balancing agent. Notice how Amalia makes a clear statement about how key intentions and experiences in the human body are designed to be challenging, at times, while essential to our soul's growth.

My guide, Gold, has returned. Gold is my primary guide. The soul that is on my left in my soul pod is the soul with whom I embody most often. Gold tells me that my overall purpose today is to learn to enjoy life. I am doing very well with my intention. I've had many challenging lives, so this one is meant to be enjoyed.

Gold tells me that I still stuff my emotions, particularly sadness. I need to let these feelings out when they happen and allow myself to be vulnerable. Gold says I am firm, constant, solid, and independent. It is alright that

I have just a few close people around me. I must tap more into the quiet support of a few. Plus, I am to spend more time finding my peace alone.

Gold explains I have had past lives that ended earlier than I wished. This explains, in part, why I want my current life to last a relatively long time. As I allow myself to feel fear and sadness, it will be easier to release these emotions as my life progresses.

Gold holds up a mirror for me to sense the color my soul emanates: gold ringed with dark burgundy red. I have incarnated primarily on earth. I can tap Gold's energy when wearing gold jewelry and clothing.

•••••••

Amalia's guide is intensely supportive, as is always true for our guide. Note that Amalia's overall goal is to enjoy her current life. Most of us think our main intention is to have a specific type of work, earn a particular income, and the like. Never far from my mind is a client from years ago who was told in her regression that her purpose in life was to be a good friend. I suspect all of us would be more satisfied with our lives if we stopped judging how much we accomplish. Plus, we most likely do not take enough time for beneficial solitude.

Fears we hold frequently result from past-life circumstances. Amalia wants a long life now and has learned that she has underlying feelings from previous lives that ended earlier than optimal. Unexplained worries in life today often relate to past-life challenges. Gold reiterates that Amalia must not stuff her feelings. At the conclusion of Amalia's regression, she learns that her soul color is primarily gold. Gold indicates her soul evolution is advanced on a ten-point scale, likely an eight to a nine.

Souls like Amalia are designed to function primarily on earth. Generally, EBS find life on earth tolerable and comfortable, having experienced numerous lives in a human environment. In the following two chapters, you will learn about the unique and evolved qualities of IPS and ARS, who often are more challenged and stymied when functioning in the human arena. EBS have walked through, maybe tripping and falling, numerous lives, gaining familiarity with the complexities they may encounter.

Ask Yourself

What fears and phobias seem too expansive or unexplained in your present life and perhaps surface from past-life engagements? Be sure to honor your emotions rather than repress them.

The next EBS client finds herself at a white temple and discovers that her panel of wise elders is in this space. Generally, only an EBS has a group or panel of guides, which is always a clue for me as I begin a soul regression. They are described as sitting in robes on the floor in this regression, an uncommon experience as these lofty experienced souls generally are seated at a robust and important-seeming table facing the client.

LOUISE: Realizations During a Council Meeting

I have been in lives before where it was easy to be myself. I have chosen this life to be complicated. I will have to work to be true to myself. Others will not see that I am different from them. I will find my group once I discover and honor who I am. Because I'm LGBTQ today, I must honor and not avoid my true self. I must propel myself, on my own, out of the situations I was born into with others who are not like me.

•••••••

We are intentional when we preplan a life that will not be easy. If you were sitting across from me, you might now ask, "Why don't we just choose smooth, effortless lives?" We could say, "No pain, no gain." But did you gain a sense of self-esteem and skill automatically? I don't think that is true for most if not all of us.

Louise reflects on the benefit of having to dig in and not be afraid to be authentic. We might say, "Don't hide your light under a bushel basket." Authenticity asks, or even demands, our human culture to grow. Being clones of one another does not instigate expansion and evolution. Scripting an upcoming incarnation where our family members and neighbors have been entrenched for generations in a particular lifestyle does not mean we must adopt our family's mentality. For example, let's say no one in your family has made their living as a musician. Your ability and passion happen to reside in the musical world. Do you deny the truth of who you are? Or do you honor yourself? Louise is a supreme example of being who you are.

> *When I find the light in myself, I will know it in others. I was born of good people who are on a different wavelength. I have found my group, but we must become a team. When we get together, we will make a beacon. I have chosen in this life to be very mental, so I must work hard not to forget about the heart.*
>
> *There are four or five on my council of elders. We are all in robes, sitting on the floor. This life is exciting and energetic as I find my true self. It will be fun and not dull. We will be assertive and self-directed. We might even learn how to play. I haven't let my light shine yet; I have taken life and its happenings too seriously.*

• • • • • • •

We must discover who we are at the core. Louise has realized she is different than her family. As she acknowledges to herself and the outside world who she is and what makes her happy, then, and only then, will she find her people. Group energy can advance our culture from a narrow perspective of who we should be to a boundless understanding of what values and behaviors are healthy versus strange and frightening.

To underscore a principal skill, we must embrace being both a soul and a human; a head without a heart or a heart without a head can easily lead one astray. Hopefully, I have emphasized through this regression the importance of the essential head-heart balance.

Again, Louise gives us a sign she is an EBS with her council of three or more members. Another interesting aspect in this soul regression is her comment that she sits on the floor with her teachers' panel. This gives me a critical indication that Louise is an advanced soul, or she wouldn't find herself seated on the floor in a relaxed fashion along with her primary guide team. When finding her true self, we hear vital descriptors such as *exciting*, *assertive*, and *self-directive*. Look for what is enjoyable in your life and be the boss of your life. Additional key elements for a progressive life include not being too serious and being sure to play.

Soul regression reveals the power of truth in shaping how we are to live an evolutionary embodiment. Take note of Louise's visit with her council. Simultaneous to living daily life as a human is the activity of our HS that is happening in the spiritual realm. While we make routine choices in our daily lives, at the same time we are active as an EBS, consulting with our guides and carrying the responsibility to coordinate with the higher realm to benefit humanity.

> *The abuse I suffered as a child is not my story. We are not to get caught up in the story of each life. We must remember who we indeed are as a soul. If I am not fearful, my light is brighter. In past lives, I could retreat and be solitary; I do not have that option in this life.*

•••••••

What is a story, and what is real? Your story means you don't massage your traumas and often say to yourself, "Poor me." Remember you are a soul advancing with each accomplishment and contributing to humanity's needs. I suggest you massage the people and activities you're passionate about. If the word *massage* doesn't resonate, think about someone rubbing your back; it feels so good, as opposed to having a badly bruised knee and complaining about it rather than helping it heal.

There is powerful learning to be gained during a lifetime when we align with our soul's truth. It is often our most difficult lives, where we are challenged not to become stuck or blinded by the complexity of life circumstances involving physical disorders or the behavior of others, that provide the most notable progress.

Earth-Based Souls: Ongoing Lives to Aid Humanity

As life on earth began to develop civilizations, a conglomerate soul group arrived in body and pledged to advance human culture. Members of this expansive group, with innumerable examples, had been incarnating elsewhere in the universe. One soul illustration stands out (remember to step away from religious dogma in your thinking). What I call the Moses soul has been in body on earth, taking crucial steps to activate human understanding and behavior at the highest level. The soul of Moses was also Mahatma Gandhi and Nelson Mandela. Critical news journalists, political figures, and simply your next-door neighbor are examples of the Moses soul who can be embodied as more than one person simultaneously. *Split incarnation* is the term that defines concurrent lives. The Moses soul is always an agent of change in their role to alter human action.

Jim, our next soul regression client, describes choosing a portion of soul energy to invigorate his incarnation and the result of his selection. This soul energy perspective includes details of how split incarnation is managed energetically.

JIM: Choosing the Portion of Soul Energy to Bring

My guides tell me that I brought 31 percent of my soul essence into life today. They recommended that I bring more because of the demands of my prebirth blueprint. I was arrogant and thought I could manage just fine with 31 percent. Because my soul color is bright blue, indicating advanced soul capability, my guides let me choose how much to bring. I should have listened.

My guides tell me that is how we learn and that I will do everything right. They say to hang in there, and they will help me. Now they take me to the hall of records, where the archives of my past lives are held. I am here to remind myself that my current life was planned because I needed more experience on earth, even though I thought I knew all I needed to know. Now I want to learn more about those souls who are the librarians in the hall of records in spirit. There is special training for the librarians because they don't just get the books for you; they comment on specific past lives. They can be accommodating if we listen to what they have to say.

•••••••

Soul regression unveils the details of how and why we select a particular percentage of our soul energy to bring into our body to accomplish our prebirth plan. Jim states, *I should have listened*, which indicates he is unlikely to ignore the advice of his guides in future lives. His guides will assist him as he moves through his embodiment in more ways than can be explained. Instances of his guides' support could include orchestrating certain souls to come into Jim's life to be of benefit, providing Jim with frequent intuitive guidance to navigate his life, and increasing Jim's energetic bond with his HS to progress with his life goals.

Jim often stops in the archival past-life library during soul regressions. An experienced EBS who serves as a librarian can indicate accomplishments already achieved, such as being a devoted spouse or friend, and what else we need to attain while climbing the evolutionary ladder. Withstanding grief and loss are a prime example.

> *Because I am a more advanced soul, I was allowed to step into my current life without more soul energy. I should have been more cautious and observant. They think I have seen the light—meaning I'll be a good exhibit for others when they choose how much soul essence to bring. Splits can happen, but my guides must consider the circumstances planned for both concurrent lives. Then they will advise the soul on how much energy to bring for each split life.*
>
> *Higher beings always observe embodied souls under stress, like me, with my amount of soul energy. The guides want to understand the pessimistic attitude that can happen. They will support me to get through my present life. In addition, guides can advise other souls about how much soul essence to bring for each incarnation.*

•••••••

Perhaps it is surprising how the higher realm and our ongoing soul evolution function as the school of life, where our embodied encounters and trials and tribulations not only serve our expansive needs but also aid the growth of others around us. As our guides examine the master plan for an ensuing lifetime, they advise us about how much soul energy we bring to earth. Soul regression is both an art and a science. In other words, the advancement of our soul must be both mental and emotional. Head and heart must function alongside one another.

Jim's session broadens our perspective about souls in spirit and the leeway to choose free will. As EBS, we learn that our guides will allow us to take on particularly taxing life experiences since we've gained the fortitude over many lives to manage complex life events. The learning is multifaceted. Even at the soul level, we can be headstrong, believing we can cope yet discovering we're on the edge of our abilities. Soul learning can be gained, both during and after an incarnation, from our tenacity that enabled us to manage stressful life choices such as health issues, relationships, and the like. Or we may realize that we have overloaded our life plan and will consider this in future lives. Also, our guides function in a learning mode of how much free choice to allow us and where to draw the line.

The hall of records and the role of the librarian fascinates Jim. Though not explained by his guides, I surmise that Jim's HS suspects it will be tapped for an upcoming responsibility relative to the energetic repository of all past lives. Finally, Jim's guides expand our understanding of the delicate balance of soul essence when a split incarnation happens. Guides cautiously examine the commitments and intricacies of our split-life blueprints to ascertain the feasibility of two simultaneous lives and the necessity of sufficient life force for each incarnation.

Ask Yourself

What taxing agreements did you accept in your life today? Are you willing to persevere with health issues, complex relationships, and more because you are advancing your soul evolution and that of your HS?

Prepare to take in the following client regression narrative as a powerful example of an EBS who agreed to influence misnomers and misunderstandings concerning gender and religion: how men or women should behave, which religion is correct and paramount, and the soul of Mother Mary, who is not necessarily tied to dogmatic religion but is a powerful guide. As you read, consider how many assumptions we make as humans that may or may not be accurate.

THOMAS: Body Pain to Quiet the Mind

I am in my mother's womb not long before birth. I feel strong emotions that are like a big storm. I feel like I am the wrong sex; I feel feminine, but I am not. Now I understand that I have opted for this conventional portal through the male body. My life will be about the development of the feminine in the male. This will help others know that men can be soft, open, and connecting. I do not have to follow the traditional way society thinks men should be.

I am a priest in a long black robe with buttons down the front. My hair is dark brown and long; I'm in my thirties. I feel serene as I stand on a hill gazing at the harbor; this seems like Italy. I am prayerful and contemplative as I feel serenity, the divine, and gratitude.

I am not ashamed; I am like a conduit without inhibition. There are Muslims here. I see buildings on either side of the channel. I see mosques below me. I deeply appreciate the group of us that are part of my order. We are not like traditional Christians; we are separate. I don't want to leave, but I have a duty to fulfill. I adore these infrequent moments alone. My group is unique.

•••••••

Crucial to humanity's evolution yet unfulfilled is the consciousness and balance of divine feminine and masculine qualities. Thomas has agreed to demonstrate and propel the acceptance of not labeling qualities as male or female; such names are misnomers. Let's just put it bluntly: Making assumptions about the capabilities or behavior of men or women, or people based on their culture, is inappropriate. We are not ashamed of who we are at the core; we are calm, centered, and grateful. Thomas belongs to a group of Christians who are neither dictatorial nor judgmental.

My skin is deep brown or dark complexioned. I come from the Middle East. Now I am in Jerusalem in a church. It is dark, with lots of candles. The feel is reverent and mystical. This is a holy day that is joyous and full of connection. I am doing what I do best. I offer love to them all. The people have olive skin; the women wear scarves. There are little children, and most of these people are poor.

This is not a large church, and I do not dominate. It's just the people and me. They feel cared for with joy. I wear a long dark robe and am bearded. I feel profoundly humble.

I am older now, alone in my bedroom, with gray hair. I'm sick and won't be here much longer. I wear a long white nightgown. I must get out of bed to do something. This is the twelfth or thirteenth century. I am not supposed to leave my room because people get excited to see me. I get them all stirred up, and they realize they have the power to change things.

Now I discover that the door to my room is locked. I'm held captive because I disturb those in power. Yet people want to be near me because I show them the way. I know that I will be hanged. I am in the square now. The people are screaming, "Stop!" Those who will kill me have spears and funny metal helmets with pointy tops resembling sailboats. They have darker skin than mine.

My hands are tied behind my back. I'm not afraid. This is not the end because of what I know. It is so sad that it has come to this. Pure love, not anger, changes all of this. They hang me. Now, I feel like a cloud. I'm satisfied because I made a difference by touching people's hearts and opening them to what is real. I allowed the women to be part of the church. This was not supposed to be, but it was remarkable for the women. Perhaps I was executed for helping the women. I was a Christian not associated with the church. It was the time of the Crusades.

I'm in the spiritual realm in the golden city. It is so good to be home. I absorb the streams of light here. My soul guide is tied to the energy of the divine feminine. My guide told me I could call her Mother Mary, Isis, or Kwan Yin. She adds that peace, joy, and love must be taught, not anger and war.

I am shown my soul color as deep, rich blue. My life purpose is to break free of tradition and dogma. Mother Mary tells me I do this well because it comes from the heart. She continues, "Of late, you have been distracted.

You started to write but stopped. You know what to say, but pretend that you do not."

When I feel fear and anxiety, I've disconnected from my soul knowing. Mother Mary tells me that I forget who I am. She tells me all I must do is look at her and sense her with my intuition. I get caught up in the facility of my mind and must learn to let this go.

The physical pain I am facing is about feeling incomplete. That life was serene. This current life is much more demanding. The pain is a distraction for your mind; it is a thought form that causes you to focus on the present moment. I am told I ruminate too much and must learn to be in the moment.

I am to play with the energy of my heart and tap into the expansiveness that I am. In the past life, I connected heart to heart with the purity of who I am. I am to be brave with courage, emanate what I know, and stop thinking my awareness sounds crazy.

My soul ray is seven (the alchemist). Mother Mary is related to Master Saint Germaine, lord of ray seven. The divine mother touches my chakras to help balance me. Ray seven is all about the equilibrium of all energies.

•••••••

Consider the critical components of Thomas's life blueprint. The headline for Thomas's life today is to be in a male body to teach the following construct: Gentleness and humility are divinely inspired and not gender specific. Thomas is to live his true nature, whether in a male or female body. The energy of Mary, Kwan Yin, and Isis as master guides defines compassion and forgiveness. Don't be fooled and assume this divine feminine energy is soft and quiet. Yin is also strong and intentional.

Thomas lived as a priest whose orientation was mystical, in alignment with the early Christian teachings, pre-350 BCE, when reincarnation and immortal consciousness were taught rather than the idea of ascension to heaven after one lifetime. In his current life, Thomas was employed in corporate America for a lengthy period, falling captive to the intensity and ego of his industry. Chronic pain forced him to be in the stillness of now, stepping away from left-brain authority to relax his body and lessen physical pain.

Thomas's guides point him to care for others in his healing practice, maintaining the knowledge that we are all equally important. Ray seven is the alchemy of all divine energy merged into one and honored to serve as the crucible for earth's egalitarian future.

In Summary

If you are a spiritual EBS who has chosen to read this book, you are likely a soul at a level of at least six or seven on the ten-point scale. In combination, your earth past lives, the guidance of your HS (even if you feel you are not consciously aware of the guidance), and aspects of your present life are what point you toward being an EBS or not. Continue through chapters 5 and 6 before you assess your soul's origin and essence. Keep communing with your HS, give it a name, and be open to ascertaining if you are EBS, IPS, or ARS. Once you know your soul type, accepting your life intentions and events will be easier.

Things to Think About

- Though you may find various human actions less than desirable, as an EBS you enjoy life on earth more than you do not. Also, you likely have relatively few severe or chronic health issues.
- You are motivated to assist humanity's evolution in small and not-so-small ways.
- You have clues, or more than clues, about past-life details with souls in your current life, eras of time that interest you, and global locations that you are drawn to.

Homework to Determine if You Are an EBS

1. Do your best to trust your suspicions about past-life details.
2. Practice writing a dialogue with your HS.
3. What elements of your current life do you need to accept rather than avoid or wish would go away?

CHAPTER FIVE

Interplanetary Soul Gifts, Challenges, and Purpose

> I don't belong on earth; my soul is from the stars. I'm visiting earth for a while to help people listen to their hearts.
>
> —NIKKI ROWE

IPS, in small numbers, agree to embody on earth to enhance our human culture. IPS are not designed for life on earth and often grapple with health and emotion-based challenges. Intestinal, skin, neurological, and autoimmune issues are experienced by IPS. Intuition is frequently acute for these sometimes isolated people whose advanced insight into beneficial ways of life is apparent. IPS know they are purposeful on earth. Relatedly, coping with living within the human body and facing unwholesome human behavior can be troubling for them.

The Nature of Interplanetary Souls

Advanced souls from non-earth locations have been influencing humanity's development by guiding souls on earth or incarnating in earth bodies. I refer to such souls as IPS. IPS who embody on earth are highly skilled because of the culture from which they originate. Generally, IPS come from celestial locations within our solar system, including earth. Occasionally, souls from the Milky Way galaxy are embodied on earth.

Approximately 1 to 2 percent of humans are IPS. Please support this small number of IPS souls on earth. Spiritually oriented people are always rather experienced souls, with a half being either IPS or ARS. Source or divine energy has persevered over tens of thousands of years to guide humanity to greater levels of evolution. One way to transform the less functional earth lifestyle has been through the periodic uptick of IPS born on earth.

Relatively early in my thirty years of guiding soul regression, I began to work with numerous clients who discovered during their sessions that they were IPS. When I asked my guides why they sent so many IPS for regression to gain insight into their non-earth origin, I was told that many IPS are challenged to function on earth in the human body. Most IPS have contended with more than fifty earth lives, while a fair number of IPS have been on earth fewer than ten times.

Often, IPS cope with physical and emotional obstacles. To list a few, allergies, digestive issues, autoimmune disorders, autism, ADHD, and vision issues. On the flip side, IPS without exception are highly skilled in various ways, such as in music, art, technology, intuition, writing, and more. A broad reference for regression narrative and explanation about the life and benefit of IPS on earth is my book *Souls on Earth*.

Chronic illness is common for an IPS. At the same time, it is a teaching tool for both the person coping with such health challenges and the others around them. Allison's experience may be eye-opening as it is descriptive of what IPS often face.

ALLISON: Lessons Learned from Chronic Illness

Allison is in her early twenties and was diagnosed with diabetes in her middle teens. At the time of her between-lives soul regression, she had become legally blind as a complication of her chronic illness. One of Allison's critical questions during her between-lives soul regression was, "What is the reason for having to move through such severe physical issues?"

It is hard for me to take physical form. Each time I do, it is easier. I came to earth this time to stick it out, to be here, and not to try to escape. I have come to earth four or five times. I get sick so I can feel my body. This lets me know I am still here and must laugh and enjoy happiness. I need to love and not fear that my happiness will disappear.

My vision issues are to help me let go of my ego and live with humility and compassion. I become too attached to the physical (corporeal) part of life. I must spend more time going inward. Going inward is my home. My home is close.

Earth is not my home. I came to experience the physical form here. I came for the separation from where I truly belong. I came here for the first time five thousand years ago. I have lived in other places (galaxies and dimensions). Here, the veil is thicker. You forget more when you come here. If you did not forget, you would not want to stay. What I am going through is complex and will give me growth and understanding.

The spiritual realm gives me strength. I am moving toward becoming an elder. My council of elders is cheering me on. They say I make it more complicated than it needs to be. I do not trust them easily. I am told to trust them and that they will never leave me. I am told to eat more raw foods and to walk more. They also tell me to meditate more. I need to love my body more. Now I am being massaged by light. It feels freeing.

•••••••

From an earthly vantage point, Allison could be pitied for her ailments and inability to live a normal life for someone her age. Examining her life from the soul's perspective provides a distinctly different understanding of her plight.

Rather than feeling sorry for Allison, we can appreciate that people's life circumstances are put in place to give the soul a chance to reach higher or more profound levels of spiritual wisdom. She has a golden opportunity in her present life to go beyond the ego, focus on deeper spiritual concerns, and serve as a mirror for the advancement of many others. Many girls her age would be simply materialistic.

Allison describes herself as a soul who has been in human form only a few times. Based on multiple regression accounts, many souls of advanced standing have experienced incarnation in dimensions and physical locations other than on earth. Such souls appear to have amassed significant soul knowledge before embodying on earth.

Allison must connect with her guides more frequently to absorb their direct support. She will discover that being in an earth body is facilitated when she follows the recommendations of her supportive souls in the higher realm and walks, eats, and meditates as they request. A fundamental rule of thumb for IPS and all experienced souls on earth is to stay tuned in to their HS and guides continuously.

Ask Yourself

Do you, or someone you know, cope regularly with a complex health issue such as serious digestive issues, ADHD, or an autoimmune disorder? Chronic and difficult-to-treat physical issues are often an indication of being an IPS.

Kyle, my next IPS client, was raised in a middle-class Christian family where his father was a minister. He holds a highly responsible business development position in a specialized large company. Prepare to learn how IPS can incarnate to impact culture and leave their bodies when needed with ease (circumstance that no longer happens in our contemporary times).

KYLE: Yin and Yang Guides for an IPS

I'm out in the desert with sand all around me. I notice multiple pyramids around me. This is a city, in a sense. It's a desert city. People are nearby, but not beside me. I'm wearing sandals that are made of fiber, with what seem to be male feet. My skin tone is more on the dark side. The trousers I'm wearing are loose and have a tan-colored drawstring waist. My tunic shirt is loose.

There are rings on both my hands. I have very black curly hair, large eyes, and a humanlike face that seems Middle Eastern. Now I notice my dark eyes are more prominent than normal human eyes.

I smile as I walk home or to a place where I know others. Now I am standing in front of a triangular building. There's only one entrance since the rest of the building seems to go into the hillside. It's as if there's a natural cave as part of the building.

I step inside, with only natural light that comes through the door window. There's a fire going in the room with lanterns in corners. I notice carpet around the fire and on the walls. I sit by the fire, and a few others are in the room. A woman brings me a cup of tea. She is my wife. My mother is also in the room.

There's a calm in the room, while something outside is troubling. I am not from this area. I came to help in some way. I've inserted myself into this community but am not one of them. I've come to witness something. I'm not from this planet, but I came into this body to bear witness to what is or will occur. This is earth, but it is much earlier than now. There are pyramidlike structures.

• • • • • • •

As you read Kyle's regression narrative, what was your first that he is an IPS? Those larger-than-normal eyes stood out initially. Thousands of years ago, an IPS could choose to embody as an adult human immediately and then dematerialize from that corporeal form. To reiterate, IPS like Kyle have been arriving on earth and elsewhere to expand humanity's evolution for a long time.

It's a bit later. I see a plaza with pyramidal structures around it. I see fireballs falling from the sky and lighting up the land around me. People are running around and very concerned about what is happening. Someone comes and holds on to me. They are frightened as we see what looks like comets. I think we should run into the building where I had been. A tunnel at the back of the building goes down into the earth. It is a safe place to get away from the danger that is occurring on the surface.

There's a staircase that leads down. I go down and enter another room for safety. We use a large stone to block the doorway. There are various rooms down here where people wait to see what will happen on the surface. We're all aware that something destructive has happened. We may have to be in this underground city for many years. The rest of that past life I spent underground.

Now it's the last day of my life. I don't age in this life. I know when my time is done. I'm sitting in a cross-legged position and preparing myself to leave my body and ascend. I close my eyes, take deep breaths, and feel myself rise out of my body. I go into a light. I float upward.

It's all light here. I pop through a barrier as I rise. I'm now in a vast, clean, stark temple complex. I'm in a marble temple that is so large I feel like I'm outside. The ceiling is so high that I almost can't sense where it is. Yet I know I'm inside a structure.

Others come to greet me. They're glad to see me. They invite me to sit at a table and talk about my experiences in the life I just completed. It's so tranquil here. This is a place of learning. A male and a female energy sit to talk with me. Their clothing appears to be loose white robes.

I find myself flickering in and out of the body I had in the life I just completed. These two want to know more about what happened in my past life and how I feel about the experience. It was a good life but frustrating because so many people couldn't understand what would occur. I somehow knew what was going to happen in advance. I was there to help people with the changes that would occur. It was hard because people thought I was strange. They knew I wasn't one of them. I was different because of my looks. I had rather large eyes. I carried myself in a different way than the people who lived there.

•••••••

Kyle had agreed to aid an earth community where there was prior knowledge that a bombardment of comets would cause destruction. The group of people seemed to have difficulty accepting Kyle because he appeared very different from them. Though this description may sound odd, based on my experience guiding IPS clients a considerable time ago, such events as comets and non-earth souls arriving for assistance were regular. Once again, note that dying as an IPS in that early time was like breath to no breath.

The critical point is that wisdom from non-earth cultures has been intended to assist humans and other beings for longer than we can recount. In today's life just as thousands of years ago, IPS are misunderstood and, to some degree, ignored because they look or act differently than the majority.

These two who are with me feel pleased with my performance. I feel a loving, supportive energy from them. They are what I call yin and yang guides. The female guide I have seen in my dreams. I call her Elizabeth, and she is blonde. The male has silvery dark hair. He feels old, wise, and authoritative. She is more sympathetic and loving.

First they want to take me to a cleansing room where I bathe in this shower of golden light that cleanses on a soul level. I'm clearing any negative energy from that past life. Then I'm clothed in a loose, golden caftan-like garment.

•••••••

Pay attention to the essential partnership of a heart-centered, female-energy guide and a more mental, male-seeming guide, who create remarkable balance. Our human lives require such symmetry and a healthy perspective. Cleansing of residual negative energy from a client's past life occurs spontaneously in approximately 60 percent of all my soul regressions. Cleansing is provided when a client's guides and HS deem it essential. The wisdom of guides is often breathtaking.

The two of them now sit me down. They're ready for questions. The male energy guide says his name is Baal. Where we are now is my home location where my HS resides. This is a physical planet in the sixth dimension. The souls from this location look at larger pictures of soul history. We try to influence larger goals of collective souls to aid their journeys toward more significant expansion and integration into the one, the Source of all. The purpose is to assist societies where souls travel and exist. It's like a river and a tapestry where one can touch and psychically influence the progress of raising vibrations of various cultures in the universe. We are to guide advanced souls back to the one.

The past life I discovered is a place like earth, but not earth, many billions of years ago. A society there had some advanced knowledge of living and building technologies. That group inevitably had to go underground because that planet had to shift into a new paradigm. Those entities went below to hide and wait to see if the new world would be one where they could exist.

My two guides say they are members of a council they check with, occasionally between lives, to discuss other locations where there may be a need for my embodiment. We also consider what would be best for the spirit of my soul. Baal and Elizabeth provide primary guidance for my soul. I am told that I've had a few dozen earth lives.

•••••••

Baal and Elizabeth have ushered Kyle to his home location in the celestial realm. Most IPS visit the locale where their HS resides during the soul regression experience. Rejuvenation and remembrance upon their arrival at home tap into an emotional awareness of reality and familiarity that is nearly inexplicable.

It is nearly impossible to describe the power of what soul regression clients come to realize. To support the expansion and integration of societies where souls exist is a high priority; IPS can impact the progress of various cultures through action and energetic effect. Simultaneously, Kyle must absorb what is revealed in his regression and take his responsibility seriously, but not take himself seriously. Having had a few dozen earth lives is a minimal number.

It is clear that Kyle was incarnate somewhere other than earth, where life may have been overly focused on science and technology. Ultimately, this non-earth culture had to literally and figuratively go underground to resurface with a new approach to their culture. I trust that the intricacy of attaining a healthy life anywhere in the universe is complex and falls on the shoulders of how the members of any location operate their daily living.

In life today, I intend to be an example and a peacemaker to show love and comfort around me. Also, demonstrate how to move through a human existence without creating heavy karma or getting caught in emotional entrapments. My guides tell me I have experienced trauma that has created psychological blocks, causing me to judge myself and others. I am to release this and let go of how I or others should be. Accept what is. Know that it's part of the creator's plan. All are lessons to move through and not stay in. You are forgiven for all you fear. You've done nothing wrong.

I am to trust my guides will keep me safe on this journey. They tell me to teach what I know. I am to find a like-minded community that understands me. I'm advised to get out of my way and trust my impulses. I will be a light for others. The right connections and paths will be revealed. I am not to fear.

• • • • • • •

Kyle's soul regression exhibits critical factors of the history of the universe where sudden energetic and lifestyle alterations can occur. Guides explain that when an IPS is embodied on earth, it is essential to avoid creating karma and emotional impediments. Kyle has absorbed trauma in his current life that must be released. It can burden an experienced soul, such as an IPS, and they need to not take on the negative energy of being human or judge human behavior. Now that you have absorbed the specifics of my client's revelation, I urge you to utilize what you've read, using heart and head. We all become caught, at times, in karma and emotional entrapments. I implore you to let go of what does not serve.

Ask Yourself

Do you sense that you were incarnated in a very early time on earth or somewhere that was not earth? Or that you impacted these places from the soul level?

IPS embodied on earth have much to model to the general population of earth beings, as the need and worth of these wise souls come online. Our terrestrial environment is the most dense and complex location in our solar system, and hence the one where we have the most excellent opportunity to progress rapidly as a soul. Physical, emotional, and spiritual challenges in our current life are often explained through the discovery of having lived in a reality other than, and dramatically different from, that of earth. This revelation creates a sense of relief for many clients, and the understanding involved opens the door to developing a more effective coping ability. IPS often feel out of place on earth, yet they are sorely needed.

CASSIE: Serving as a Container to Purify Others' Energy

I'm in my mother's womb, and it is not long before my birth (into my current life). I have a strong body that must last a long time. At age fourteen, I must learn to allow certain people's energy to move through my body without blocking it. I'll be able to pick up people's energy easily and feel their pain to make it better. This will only work if there aren't blockages. I purify others' energy. I can feel it and transform it if there is a smooth flow.

I'm new at this, but it is hard. I wanted to do this because it is essential. People on earth get stuck quickly. I can do this well, but it is more challenging here on earth because the issues are more complex. People are confused because they often don't understand their lives from the bigger picture. Also, I had to do a lot of preparation for the body so that it could purify the energy of others.

•••••••

As an IPS, Cassie has arrived on earth with the ability to serve as an energetic purifier for others. She must avoid her blockages, as well as not draw in and hold the energy of others. Cassie is a bit like a cleansing station; humans quickly become bogged down on earth, likely because they do not comprehend the bigger picture of the soul. It is moderately common for a soul to handle body and brain modifications in the womb.

In a past life, I see I'm alone in a cold damp room with plaster walls. My shoes are wooden and weird, and I'm wearing leggings, a skirt, and a black peacoat. I'm a little girl, about five years old, with brown ponytails.

I don't like it here; people do not get along very well. An old woman lives in this house with me. She's so tired and is my grandmother. I try to be quiet so I don't bother her. I play with wooden pegs, circles, and shapes, but I'm bored and want to leave.

It's later now. I'm married, and we argue a lot. We have little money and share a house with his family. The work is hard; there's handwashing, cleaning, and cooking. There should be more of a point to this life. My husband is distracted with his politics. He gets out often, and I stay home most of the time.

Now I'm in bed; I'm old. There's a friendly maid, but my kids and grandkids don't care much about me. My husband has died. I've been alone for such a long time. I'm having breathing issues.

I've died and see many points of light. This feels so much better. My body is gone. It is so hard to be alive; it's tedious and unusual for me. I would describe it as unnatural to be in a life like that when you must be stuck. Now, I love being free.

The old woman in the past was my grandmother and is the same soul as my husband today. I was to learn more patience in that life. I am to accept that people are not perfect, and I need patience with them. The past-life circumstances were much worse than in my life today, yet I have similar feelings today. In my current life, I often feel everything is heavy. I don't like to come back into an earth body, but it is getting a little easier in each life on earth. I need the willpower to keep going.

•••••••

Cassie's past life contained unhappiness and a lack of love and support. IPS who arrive on earth come from home locations where everyday life is healthy and supportive. An IPS who has not walked through many earth lives will find it cumbersome to face the lack of emotional balance they know from their familiar home turf. Often, IPS are entirely caught off guard by the way humans function.

To alter the past life's lack of moral support, the grandmother soul has returned to Cassie in her current life as her spouse, a common occurrence. Life on earth is, in many ways, utterly opposite to life at an IPS home. Patience is the key. Cassie must be accepting and persevering to accomplish her human intent. For souls unfamiliar with earth life, daily living feels like swimming upstream.

Now I have moved into the spiritual realm between my lives. I'm floating, and it feels like the sky. I'm with five to ten people, or souls, now. It's not earth here. They are simply shapes. We're all listening and learning about life. We have semiphysical form; we have shape but not form. We practice things like bouncing energy, which is emotion. We're learning how to take in energy and bounce the emotions away from us.

I see my son, Nick, who is eight years old; he's practicing with energy too. A teacher or coordinator is helping us learn patience as we practice. This skill takes a long time to learn. To master it, you must play with the energy and be patient, just like practicing a musical instrument. The teacher is a specialist who has been in an earth body before but no longer.

•••••••

One of Cassie's soul skills is to separate from the emotion often attached to the energy that humans exude. In this manner, we can benefit from the power of others without taking on unwanted feelings that do not belong to us. Cassie's young son comes from her celestial domain and is being trained to handle energy by the guide or coach of this IPS locale.

Now we're being shown people on earth. They have a hard time remembering what they came to do on earth. They have so many burdens. You must have these burdens in life on earth to learn empathy and patience. Then you can diffuse the burdens. When you are in a body, it can seem heavy and depressing. From my vantage point in the spiritual realm, what is essential and not seems obvious. Life in the body is very constrictive, and being here is light and sound. People forget to show love. They suffer and do not think because it is hard to remember what you are supposed to do.

I'm told that right now, I have some energy intrusions. These dark spots in my human energy field need to be released. My doubt and low self-esteem allow these intrusions to happen. I need to focus on receiving purification to remove these dark spots. All I must do is take a brief meditation or relaxation, and my guides will provide a golden-white light that scans my body for intrusions. I ask for this, and it happens.

My guides find that my heart is most clogged; they remove the blocked energy. More souls are being sent to earth to do the energy work I can do. Many people on earth who can purify people's energy are young, from babies to young adults. They are very telepathic, with fewer barriers.

•••••••

Cassie's regression commentary is crystal clear as her guides explain the obstacles of human incarnation. Everyday life on earth with multiple distractions leads many souls, especially IPS, to lose sight of their life purpose. Seeing beyond our burdens gives us more remarkable patience and acceptance of life. Demonstrating love versus getting caught in the web of human frailty helps us not lose sight of who we are as a soul and remember why we agreed to incarnate.

Doubt and low self-esteem have led Cassie to have energetic holes in life today. Just asking our guides to help us cleanse the unhealthy energy we're carrying will lead to lightness and freedom. Cassie must allow her heart to be cleared of negative energy. The higher realm continues to encourage more IPS to embody on earth. These souls are often young people who are telepathically open and pure. Such souls must be supported and protected.

I've been on earth a few times, but not enough to be comfortable. I underestimated how difficult it would be on earth. It helps me know I am not used to it here on earth. My guides tell me I should not try to fix things for people. Let people work things out for themselves. I knew it would be hard to find people like me on earth, that it would be lonely. It's tricky and challenging once we are in a body because our human mind is so inadequate. What we understand about the soul level is just an approximation because we think linearly. We think in terms of structure, form, and color. Those in my soul group are purple with blue edges.

•••••••

Cassie has minimal experience on earth, leading to more significant trials in the human body. If less than 2 percent of humanity was like you, you would likely be challenged to find others with similar natures. Such circumstances could easily lead to loneliness and frustration. As an IPS in the human body, our only means of comprehension is the human brain, which is inadequate. Thus, it is critical to use intuition to stay tuned in to your HS.

> *My goal tied to being on earth is not assimilation. I am not to be at ease on earth. My purpose is to expand people's opportunities through change. I am a catalyst.*

•••••••

Cassie prepares her body to take in the energy of others for purification energetically. Her soul regression reveals that she must accept that she is not in alignment with many humans but must remain in sync with her soul agreement to aid others' evolution. Many gifted healers of today have their roots and learned their skills in their IPS home base. EBS, over many lives, have become accustomed to the challenges of earth bodies and how people on earth treat one another; IPS souls often struggle with being on earth and assimilating sufficiently to satisfy the goals of their life blueprint.

Increasingly, IPS, who bring an air of equality and holistic life from their home base, are encouraged to reside on earth because of our dire need for interdependence on earth. Catalyzing change defines the service work of IPS in human culture.

One final IPS regression client, Sallie, comes next. Not much can surprise me after nearly thirty years of guiding regression, but what you are about to learn expanded my soul knowledge exponentially. Sallie is a highly skilled professional with career responsibilities that can lessen the suffering of specific individuals. Before reading the upcoming soul regression content, consider young children's natural wisdom, perspective, and happy outlook, including their desire to play, eat, and delight in everyday life.

SALLIE: Child Souls on Earth

> *It's dark, and I'm outside. There are three eyes near me, just one eye for each animal: a deer, a wolf, and an owl. I feel glad they're here. My feet are bare and little. I seem to be wearing what we call a bodysuit; it is all one piece. It covers my legs, ankles, and wrists and has long sleeves. When I look at my face, I see flashing bright yellow and purple swirling. I don't think I have a head like humans do.*

I'm standing on wet rocks. Now I'm walking as I see stars and the crescent moon. I'm coming down a hill. I see something like the northern lights. I can jump in the air and get carried forward. It's like running, skipping, and then levitating. I feel delighted and can't wait to see where I'm going.

I'm going down to a village now. It's a welcoming kind of village with round buildings and pointy tops. I'm hungry and want candy. The wolf eye is back. I see a building with the light on, and I smell chocolate. I want to find someone who can tell me what to do.

•••••••

Like many IPS whom I regress, when Sallie taps into the soul level, much of what we expect in terms of average human circumstance is gone, such as the lack of a head where there is only energy. Guides can and often do show up in animal form, without posing any danger no matter the type of animal. When a client accesses a past life that is not on earth, their description of wearing a bodysuit does not mean what it would in an earth situation. Also, running and levitating above the ground signals that my client is again not on earth. Stay tuned for what the smell and craving of chocolate and candy will suggest.

Now I see a momlike soul who is purple. They don't use the term mom here. I sneak up on the house. I see a beautiful soul inside the window. I often don't see faces, but just souls that are energy. She doesn't know I'm there. She is smiling. It's night, and I don't want to intrude just now. I climb up in the tree to sleep. I am excited to meet the woman I'm to see tomorrow.

It feels like morning. I see swirling colors on a dark background. I'm still in the tree as I wait for the woman to see me and come get me. I was supposed to stay in the tree until I was found. A big, beautiful bird just landed in the tree. The bird has fantastic colors and eyes. The woman has transformed into a bird and comes to swoop me up. She is so wonderful.

Now her wings are all around me. She says, "I am here, Little Me." I know I am to be with her as she protects me. I call her Alpha Wolf. She embraces me in her wings. I'm so pleased we found each other. She wants to feed me. So we're going to go to her home. Now she's transforming into a wolf. In my life today, a wolf is my spirit animal.

She takes me to her cottage. We go inside, where she has cookies and milk for me. She wants to ensure I eat something as she sits at the table with me. She has caring, loving eyes. She explains she's one of my spirit guides because I have multiple guides. I was brought to her first because I am too scared to go anywhere unless she is with me.

I am told we must invite another guide, Ko, to come forward. Both have been with me for as long as I can remember. They've always been my most vital support. Ko arrives from up above, and she is an Indigenous elder. Now I feel so safe.

•••••••

Parenting figures ensure children are fed nutritiously; that is precisely what Alpha Wolf offers Sallie. Alpha Wolf, one of her central guides, renders protection, leaving Sallie to trust she is safe. When Ko, the Native guide, arrives, Sallie can embrace the composite comfort of her two primary guides.

It's time to travel. Alpha Wolf reverts to being a swirling energy of colors with wings. She puts me in a papoose on her back. We go flying high into the clouds. Ko will go with us.

I feel a fullness and warmth in my heart. There are tears in my eyes. I feel free and so grateful to be heading wherever we are going. Now I am very near my soul's home location. I'm told I must go alone and say goodbye to my two guides. This is difficult because I get lonesome easily.

I'm out of the papoose now and feel very little. Sometimes, I feel like I'm seven years old. At other times, I feel even younger. I float and have grown little wings as I go down into purple light. I feel the love in this place I am going. I know Ko and Alpha Wolf will be close if I need them.

I'm going through water. I have never felt so free when such amazing loving energy exists. I'm into warm air and am dancing to a drumbeat with other souls. There's a warm fire. I don't see much, but I feel all of this.

I feel the freest I've ever felt. I am told this is my IPS home locale. Many souls are letting me know they're happy I am here now. I am told that when I need guidance, I tap into my imagination, leading me to where Ko and Alpha Wolf always are. I go into my mind and open to whatever comes to me. It's my way to dream of what I need to be. Then I have something to lean into.

Here at my home base, there are older souls to take care of the numerous child souls. Some of these caretaker souls do incarnate on earth. I do not know any of these caretakers in my present life. I am told that often IPS like me, or what we call child souls, must find non-IPS incarnate souls on earth to serve in the caretaking role. We do not usually have caretakers like Ko and Alpha Wolf on earth.

Child souls like me are needed on earth more than ever because where I come from, there is so much love. I can bring big love to help others on earth. I feel so emotional right now as I feel the overwhelming love from my home base. I am told that I must exhibit my loving soul energy more, so my soul shines outwardly.

I have only a few lives on earth. I am not used to being so contained in the human body, which wears on my nervous system and affects my whole body, including my intestinal issues. I am not the only child soul on earth, but we are uncommon. You must walk through your current life's family and physical issues to learn how to plan future earth lives with greater ease.

• • • • • • •

Sallie's home location is populated by child souls, which maintains children's wonder and inquisitiveness. All child souls have elder souls to protect them and foster their expansion. Sallie's job on earth is to exude the depth of love at her home location, just as all children are to be loved as they flourish.

Sallie lacks human experience, which is highly challenging for her nervous system and physical body. She repeatedly faces complex digestive issues. In her daily life, she is learning how to operate in the body so she and other child souls can effectively plan future earth lives. Not only is there not enough caring, loving energy on earth, but the bright light of a child is also unmatched. Sallie plays an influential role on earth.

Ask Yourself

Do you have a unique characteristic, like Sallie, that you keep hidden from others because you fear judgment?

In Summary

The clear-sightedness of IPS is sorely needed on our planet. Earth has yet to achieve a healthy and sacred life status, including caring for all living things equally. The higher, sage intelligence of earth has opted to usher in the incarnation of more IPS to humanity in the hope of creating greater equality of life. If you are an IPS, you know how humans should treat one another. At the same time, you must care for your body, mind, and spirit in the most helpful manner for you. Please don't ignore your personal needs. As you demonstrate the most effective diet or sleep pattern for yourself, you serve as a teacher for others. Finally, you know you're different from many others, which is good. This signals to both yourself and others that you matter and are needed in our culture.

Things to Think About

- If you or a loved one feels more balanced with a specific diet, follow that diet daily.
- Your intuition and/or unique skill is essential on earth; let it shine.
- Humans do not always behave healthily; believe you are in body to advance our planet, and commit to your life intentions.

Homework to Identify Whether You or a Loved One Is an IPS

1. What are the identifying characteristics that indicate you or someone you know is an IPS?

2. If you are an IPS, stay tuned in to your HS to function more comfortably in your earth body.
3. As an IPS, you may look or act differently; you may not easily fit into everyday society, but you are here purposefully. Please value yourself.

CHAPTER SIX

Angels Among Us

When people think of angels, they think flowing robes and halos. But in the Bible, they also look like ordinary people. Why not today?

—JOAN WESTER ANDERSON

Over years of guiding soul regression clients, I made acquaintance with souls originating from the angelic realm. ARS do not embody often on earth, and many never incarnate at all. Source energy is exclusively love and compassion. ARS convey the essential energy of benevolence to earth through incarnation. Evidential signs that someone is an ARS is their acceptance of all people and lack of a critical attitude.

Planet earth, the home that provides us with a dense livable surface, began as a cloud of dust and gas. Approximately 4.5 billion years ago, earth was formed and gradually cooled to allow ocean development. Scientists suggest that human civilization began approximately fifteen thousand years ago.

Who or what is the intelligence coordinating the origin of souls on earth? What is the purpose of the angelic realm? How is it related to the overarching divine wisdom for humanity? Soul regression clients can provide knowledge about what many call God and the angelic realm.

Soul Regression Reveals Angelic Realm Souls Incarnate

Over the last twenty-five years, with multiple regression clients each week, my awareness of the nature and purpose of incarnate ARS has dramatically widened. My grasp of who or what the divine is has expanded. My gratitude to my clients and their spiritual guides is beyond measure; they educate me, one client at a time, as I seek broad-based understanding.

In keeping with the overarching theme of this book, how is it beneficial to discover you are a soul from the angelic realm? When a client realizes their soul originated in the celestial location, or the frequency labeled angelic, then their core nature and soul history surface. Attributes of angelic souls help individuals accept themselves and others and stop judging thoughts, feelings, and inclinations. Subsequently, an ARS will traverse the journey of current life, striving to accomplish their goals and be who they came into this lifetime to be, expanding individually and aiding humanity.

God is real, but not usually described the same way people describe the high wisdom of divine energy. Many ask me, "How can one person's belief about God be exactly correct while other people's perspectives are incorrect?" One client explained that the Eastern notion of gods and goddesses subdivides divine energy into various aspects.

In all my years of guiding regression, I have never had a client talk about the devil or the notion of hell. Life in body can be the most challenging circumstance as we face past-life karma, including prior incarnation freewill choices that must be balanced to evolve. As a spiritual person and a researcher of the soul, my goal is to understand the divine realm and our purpose for being.

Some believe in fallen angels, or angels cast out of heaven. Again, no client has ever described such punishment of an ARS. Human life is filled with the promotion of fear; for example, if you forget to call your mother once a week, you are somehow in trouble. All my ARS clients have agreed to embody on earth to assist humanity.

Fortunately, innumerable spiritual seekers have constructed a soul encyclopedia in my heart and mind, the repository of their spoken intuitive discoveries of who they are as a soul and why they are in the body. Begin your own data bank as I explain what to look for in the following clients' intuitive regression content. How do I discern when a client is a member of the angelic cadre? Also, how beneficial is it today to know you are an angelic soul?

Between-lives soul regression has a protocol that consists of relaxation hypnosis, past-life discovery, and accessing the client's soul or HS, assisted by a spiritual guide. Approximately a third of my clients do not uncover a past life because their guide does not consider a past life necessary. If my client travels directly to their soul level in the regression, I am 90 percent sure they are either an IPS or an ARS. I accept there is no need to learn about the small number of past incarnations that an IPS or ARS has encountered.

In-depth training and experience are critical for the regression therapist if they are to utilize their knowledge about the soul and receive intuitive direction about the client. Soul regression to the spiritual realm involves a type of language that the therapist must be able to decipher. Often, I have described the regression therapist's job as a three-ring circus: listening to the client, tapping into the therapist's intuition, and asking open-ended questions tied to soul expertise to tease out what is happening and where the client is in their regression journey. This explanation of the regression journey will become evident as you read the upcoming accounts of various clients and their eye-opening revelations.

Color serves as a specific clue to the energy and level my client has traveled to in the spiritual realm. Color connotes frequency, which relates to the energetic location, or the degree of elevation in the higher realm, that the client is experiencing during regression. To simplify this concept, think about the colors of the rainbow, from red to violet. Each rainbow color advances, step by step, to higher frequencies. Gold and pure white indicate a more advanced degree of spiritual locale than violet.

MADELINE: Many Mansions and the Great Divine Director

Madeline's between-lives soul regression gives us the flavor of the high domain where ARS reside. As you read the regression narrative, do your best to truly feel the energy of what Madeline, a woman in her seventies, discovered.

I just see light. It's a cloud with twinges of purple and blue and white. I'm walking through the cloud to purple mountains and gold over the top. There's no sense of grass or trees. I feel as if the purpleness of the mountains comes right up to me. I'm just in the purple mountain scene.

I try to walk, but I'm above the ground. The gold seems like a sun trying to come up behind the purpleness. As the golden-white light rises, I want to go toward it. Then I feel enveloped by the light. I can walk over the mountain and into the light.

It goes into a whole golden place. I sense golden mountains or golden buildings that are all sticking up. I notice points of gold light that could be beings. I am in another world. Now I need to move forward.

The ground is gold, like gold nuggets. Then I come over a bit of rise and come into a city. This is not like a human city, but it has the feel of a city. I walk into a place that feels like a holy city. I hear the words many mansions. *I am the new Jerusalem. That will not wash away. The new Jerusalem is God's kingdom on earth.*

"Hosana, Hosana in the highest, Hosana forevermore." (Dr. Backman asks, "Who is guiding this process?") I see the great divine director, who is all gold.

•••••••

To begin interpreting the content in Madeline's regression thus far, I consider what the colors blue, purple, gold, and white indicate. Instantly I know my client has traveled to an exceedingly high frequency. Madeline is "walking," but not on grounded dense energy we would consider earth. Several signs indicate that she is not consciously manufacturing her regression content. For example, most clients do not comprehend what the colors suggest. And rather than using an average pace and speaking voice, Madeline's voice is frequently soft and plodding.

The term *many mansions* seems to suggest divine lives everywhere and nowhere in particular. High-frequency evolved energy and guidance are perpetually available to each of us. I interpret God as the energy of love, compassion, and unconditional acceptance. Madeline is a practicing Christian who does not try to convince anyone else of what their beliefs should or should not be. As you absorb the ongoing elements of her soul regression, you will notice the alignment of Madeline's current-life spiritual fervor and what is unveiled about who she is as a soul.

Hosanna is an ancient term used by the Hebrews and today's Christians, signifying power and reverence for divine energy. Madeline speaks of *the great divine director*, pointing toward that expansive energy of love and compassion. Consider the account she has presented thus far and its potential meaning. How does Madeline's spontaneous regression narrative integrate and explain the interrelationship between present-life circumstances, her soul's purpose, and evolutionary history? As you absorb the content of Madeline's regression, follow my explanation of how her soul, past lives, and present life align. I invite you to keep considering, Who are you as a soul? Why are you incarnate now? What is your purpose in life today? Are you an ARS or not?

My role as a regression therapist is threefold. First, I must serve as the bus driver of the regression, meaning I keep the regression on the road and moving forward. The itinerary or content of the regression is not my role; it is the responsibility of the client's HS and spiritual guides. The therapist's skills are essential for aiding the client in using their intuition, in a relaxed state, to access specific spoken knowledge about past lives and soul content.

Second, after an in-depth interview to learn about the client's life from childhood until now, I listen without comment to the regression content as I silently consider how the client's current life relates directly to their past lives and who they are as a soul. One of the critical responsibilities of the regression therapist is to give credence to the content of the soul regression that ties directly to the client's current life.

Soul regression is a multifaceted tool that sheds light on who the client is in past lives, as a soul, and in life today. As a research modality, soul regression must provide verbalized information from the client during hypnosis that reveals the purpose of their current life, the origin of their soul, karma from past lives, past-life and present-soul relationships, and much more. Spontaneous verbal material from the client provides a case study research method, person to person, to aid in understanding the soul, life planning, emotional and physical symptoms, and extensive components of soul agreements from lifetime to lifetime.

To decipher Madeline's regression content in relation to her current life, consider that she has been very devoted to her Christian roots and church all her adult life. Despite being steadfast with her religion and related values, she does not try to force her beliefs on anyone else. In addition, Madeline is deeply committed to the people of her church and their needs. A key aspect of my client's personality is her belief that everyone is equal and should be treated respectfully. Finally, we could describe Madeline as conventional, having been married for a long time and lovingly involved with her three married children and her grandchildren. Read the upcoming narrative of her regression and think about how our souls can be reflected in our current life. I suspect you will find the revelatory details profound and valuable.

> *I am at the feet of the great divine director (GDD). He's very tall. Now the director speaks. "Oh, Madeline, thank you for coming. I love you. We've been together before. You always take on something big. I'm grateful to you. I'm sorry for your pain. I'm thankful that you do it. I want to help you because I treasure you.*
>
> *"You are a being of light. We are rather like soul mates. There is great love between us. We want humankind to know the same love. We have the same wish for evolution, that people raise themselves to the height of knowing that God is with them and in them. God wants them to see the light and be raised to be who they are as loving and loved souls. We desire that humanity does not continue gathering karma from the pain, sadness, and hurt of wars. Instead, we want humans to love each other from their souls. Then they would see no difference between them, and know that we all want the same thing for each other."*
>
> *I see a very white gown with an essence of pearliness that represents my soul energy. I am almost as tall as GDD, which means I am very tall.*

My hair is flowing. My gown is translucent with wings that seem to be part of the gown. I'm told that GDD is my primary spiritual guide.

•••••••

Critical components of Madeline's soul regression reflect her soul and human aspects. As the therapist, I am aware of my client's time-honored way of life with her religion and family, which is on the same wavelength as her advanced soul evolution and bond with God. In life today, Madeline strives to only exude kindness to those around her. Who or what does she speak of when she uses the term *GDD*?

Because Madeline spontaneously describes her gown as having wings, I hold this comment in my awareness as I wait for potential confirmation that she is an ARS. When a client describes having wings at the HS level, it is almost 100 percent the case that they are from the angelic realm. Gradually, the montage of who Madeline is as a soul and in life today gains specificity so that I can aid her in honestly knowing why she is in body today with her specific life circumstances.

The GDD, also known as the Source, God, Great Spirit, and by other labels, exudes a warmth to Madeline that is a sign of her soul-level relationship with the divine creator. My client says she is a "being of light," and that God wants the best for humans to "see the light." You may think this content sounds glorified and, perhaps, religiously dogmatic, but consider Madeline's words not as blindly devotional but as guideposts for how humanity should behave. The "hurt of war" creates karma and pain, as opposed to humans viewing one another as equals. Continue to feast on further details of Madeline's regression as you round out who she is as a soul and in life today.

Mary wants me to know that she loves me. I was her daughter in that lifetime when Christ was crucified; she knew I was absorbing more of the pain, and she wouldn't have wished for me to experience so much pain. I was so young. I went everywhere with her. I was at the crucifixion, I was at the tomb, and I was with her all the time because I was younger. I witnessed a lot more that I couldn't understand as a child. It has impacted me.

My brother Jesus was so kind; he healed them, and he did so many beautiful things, but something political got in there...and they killed him for it. Now I am crying.

•••••••

Madeline speaks of being the daughter of Mary, the mother of Jesus. Evidence suggests Mary had sons and perhaps daughters following the birth of Jesus, so Madeline's regression statement as Mary's daughter is likely valid. When a client unearths unique and profound evidence of something like being a family member of a critical soul in human history, my role as the therapist is to seek additional supportive evidence and provide discussion. (Let me note that *Jesus*, a Greek word, was the name given to that incarnate soul following the crucifixion. Jesus's actual name was Yeshua. Accounts of both Roman and Hebrew aggression toward Yeshua have been verified repetitively.) Continue to take in what Madeline details in her regression, which contains new and powerful content.

I was always afraid to stand up. I thought I was bringing forward what the Holy Spirit wanted me to do, but in past lives, I always ended up being killed...like him. I have tried to tell people the truth, but I was always killed. I guess it's why I have held back in my current life and not said as much about my true being.

Mary is giving me her hand...she says, "I'm sorry. I guess I am just... in this life...trying to understand." Politics is something I loathe. Maybe it comes from those times when I knew that Jesus's death was political. I know that when he forgave...he forgave the greater collective consciousness. I feel like I said I'd...I came down to forgive all these things.

I can do it on an intellectual basis, but when I think of the church people, I get upset again. It's always been...when they don't like your gifts...why do I care what they think? Jesus was so good, and he ended up a total failure...that's how I feel...like a failure. I thought I was a good person, and it makes me feel like a failure when people don't seem to understand me.

Now my guide wants to talk about the intention of my current life. He says, "You are so loving, and this is the most important thing. We talked to you about how hard this would be...You were so sure...your love could transform anything. It's hard down there, we know...We want you not to be afraid because we are here...You know it, but don't feel it."

•••••••

Madeline indicates that she has had past lives where she was killed for speaking her beliefs. Past-life trauma surfaces in our current life as fears, avoidances, relationships, and physical issues. Thus, Madeline often avoids speaking her honest thoughts and feelings because, in her intuitive memory, she worries about being harmed or cast aside, as happened in the past. Human history demonstrates the validity of political infighting among Romans and Hebrews during Yeshua's life, resulting in the crucifixion. Madeline's current detest for political wrangling originates in her past embodiments. When you loathe certain behavior today, ask yourself: Does my attitude arise from current life, or could it be from a past-life experience?

Madeline feels she has failed to honor her commitment to the church community. At the same time, she is baffled and distressed when her church's respected spiritual leader criticizes her love of the divine. As an ARS who shared in Yeshua's lifetime, Madeline easily slips into denigrating herself for the chosen behavior of others. ARS are tied to love and compassion in an almost inexplicable manner.

Drink in the profound direct commentary from Madeline's guide. First, the keyword *love* arises. ARS function from an inexplicable love perspective. Though I hesitate to suggest that the backbone of Madeline's angelic energy is both a blessing and a curse, I would be avoiding the inner battle within an ARS not to do so. An attitude of love can be transformative for others, but humans have free will to choose their feelings and behavior. The GDD tells Madeline that they discussed the challenge of embodying on earth as an ARS who exudes love and compassion. To paraphrase the GDD: "You know we are here, but as an incarnate soul, it is easy to become caught up in your emotions and pain in response to the human behavior around you."

Ask Yourself

Are you someone who was raised in a home where deep religious beliefs were taught? Are some of the structured attitudes of the religion uncomfortable, while you still feel a solid connection to the component of love held within religious teachings?

Recognizing Characteristics of Angelic Realm Souls

As the facilitator and witness to what my soul regression clients intuitively receive and speak, I am humbled by their wisdom. Incarnation on earth can be enormously challenging for many embodied souls who have lost sight of the higher perspective about what is the most beneficial and healthy behavior humans can demonstrate.

NATHAN: Painting Angels and Wings

Take in Nathan's experience in his regression journey of discovery as his past lives and soul nature are revealed. Like Madeline, when Nathan realizes he is an ARS he senses it suddenly; an explanation of who he truly is falls like a square peg into a square hole. Once again, the exquisite beauty of embracing one's essential qualities leads to unexplained tranquility.

I'm inside, and the temperature is comfortable. I'm alone in a room that has a dark wood floor with similar walls. My shoes are suede with a cord around the ankles, and my pants are puffy. I look like a pirate in a jacket with large gold buttons. My mustache curls on the ends like my dark wavy hair. I have on a hat with a feather in it. As a middle-aged man, I act like a smart-ass. I feel that I'm somebody, like an artist.

I'm standing with my hand on my hip. There's an oil painting on the wall with a light over it, like what you find in a museum. Now I'm walk-

ing outside feeling proud. I'm going toward a tall building with light in the windows. I don't knock and go right in. It's filled with people.

I'm in a fancy room with gold on the walls, and everyone is socializing. These are my people. I greet people around the room once I get a drink from the bar. I know I'm important. There's an important woman with a plumed hat. I like her. She doesn't look down on me but does with the crowd.

She tells me not to waste my time and life like these other people do. It's time to move forward in this past life. Now I'm in a church cathedral with burning candles. I can smell the wax. I'm in a pew by myself, praying for my sexuality to be removed. I'm too fanciful in how I dress. Others are more straightforward with their clothing, which has no feathers. I want to be more macho.

There's a light above the altar. I'm getting a no to what I've asked. I'm confused and told that I am the way I am supposed to be. I am to be okay with how I am.

I wear a painter's coat and hat in my art studio. With a palette of paint in my hand, I feel in my element in front of a canvas. I'm painting a scene with a pond and trees. There's classical music playing. I feel at peace. This is the room where I live, with a bed and a table where I eat. There's a bowl of fruit on the table. I live alone. I have candles in the window. I'm painting and humming, and I'm feeling busy and good.

It's the very last day of my life in the same room. I'm fat and lying in my bed. I'm unwell and have gray-white hair. The woman with me in the first scene is holding my hand. She says it'll all be okay, as I'm having trouble breathing.

My hat is on the table, and there's a cloth on my forehead. She helps usher me out of my body with my last breath. Thank God it's over.

This past life was good. It was complete and necessary. Yet I feel incomplete about my sexuality. Looking back on this past life now, I don't feel the sexuality. Now it doesn't seem necessary. I used to think that my sexual orientation was important when I was younger, but now I don't. Today, as a gay man, it is simply a necessary part of my personality. I do wish I was artistic now. I can't paint worth crap.

•••••••

Let us examine and dissect Nathan's discovery of his past life as a painter. One of my key responsibilities as a regression therapist is to aid my clients in uncovering the intentions of their spiritual guide. What messages and guidance for Nathan did his guide convey by presenting his past life as a gay painter? From my years as a conventional psychologist and through teaching others to guide soul regression, I know the critical importance of interviewing clients to understand their life history and current details. Questioning my client to learn who they are in their present life is essential for me to understand why their guide chooses a particular life to bring forth.

As I support my client in receiving the nudge or shove from their guide, there is always a benevolent design in what surfaces via regression. Nathan is to let go of any concern about his prevailing sexuality. Plus, he wishes he could be an artistic painter. I know Nathan well enough to say he is highly creative in other ways. Let us not lose sight of the fact that our past lives can be deeply embedded in our thoughts and emotions of today, which at times need to be let go of. Nathan's guides made it clear he was to know of his past-life challenges as a gay man, along with having artistic capabilities. He is to release all concerns about his sexual orientation at this very moment in time.

Nathan and I move forward to his between-lives soul regression, which begins with discovering a past life leading to a conscious connection with his HS. Immerse yourself in the revelation of another past life as you seek to understand what messages the spiritual guide is sending. Nathan now uncovers a life as a seemingly happily married man and father; note the soul's evolutionary balance indicated by Nathan's guides showing him two lives with different lifestyles, one as a gay man and the other in a committed straight partnership.

I'm alone outside at night in a mountain area like the Swiss Alps. I have brown boots, wool pants, a gray coat, and a fur hat. I have a rugged face with wrinkled skin and brown-gray hair. I'm an unshaven man. I'm walk-

ing on a road toward a village when I see the lights ahead. There's something I carry on my back.

Walking toward the village and the hill, I notice many log houses. I know where I'm going. I come to my house and open the door. A woman with a child are at the fireplace. I feel good to be home.

I sit down with my wife and my little boy. My wife has a bonnet with a white apron, and dinner is ready. My boy is on my lap and then crawls around my neck. Now we go to the table to eat. The silverware and plates seem like pewter.

I reach out to take my wife's hand as we look into each other's eyes. My boy is playing with his food as my wife disciplines him so that he begins to eat. She says he must eat before he goes to bed.

Now it's time to put our son to bed. I tuck him in and kiss him, leaving his door partially open. Then my wife and I sit quietly in front of the fireplace. We rock back and forth.

It's later, and I'm in a logging yard. I work with a group of men. The work is dangerous. We tie ropes around logs that are lifted on a pulley. I feel tired as I move one log and see another approaching me. I think I can grab it, and I miss it. It hits me in the head, and I have a terrible headache on the left side. I'm on the ground. A group of guys surrounds me, trying to help. My head is bleeding.

I'm just lying there. The people there prop my head and wrap my head with cotton strips. I'm not getting better. I sense that I'm fading. The noise of the conversation around me is getting less and less. I don't feel there anymore.

I can see my face. I have died. Energetically, I send love to my wife and boy. Now I feel pulling from above. I am now blue, stretchy light. I'm feeling pulled from my back, and I'm going somewhere. I'm moving through a dark area with stars toward a round opening with light. It's sort of like a stretchy tube with ripples in the walls.

• • • • • • •

Nathan, the man who died from a head injury, has completed another embodiment as he advances his soul's evolution of assisting humanity to mature and transform. Vital elements for him to absorb are that he accomplished a loving traditional family relationship. Also, he may have current symptoms of discomfort on the left side of his head, as well as worry that he will die from an injury; that is a remnant of the past and can be released. Nathan's experience of dying is easy, as is usually true in soul regression. Traveling gently, pulled through a star-filled area and toward the light, is a frequent tranquil description given by regression clients as they leave their earthly incarnation.

> *I hear music playing with pastel colors around me. I want to turn around, but I need to figure out how. First I'm sideways, and then I'm facing forward. The tube is long, and both ends are dark. I feel like I have wings, like a fish with fins flowing with the water. My wings are dark blue on the tips and lighter toward the center.*

•••••••

As noted earlier, my many years of experience guiding regression has created an encyclopedia in my mind. If during a soul regression the client describes having wings, I note this silently and continue to seek other components that may validate that my client is an angelic soul. Over many years, I have realized that the client's perception of wings is the spiritual realm's sign that I am working with an ARS.

> *As I come out of the tube, it's dark with many stars. Now I'm just there in this very vast place. I'm floating, and I feel very safe. I don't know what I'm supposed to do. Somebody is coming toward me who reminds me of Tinker Bell. This is a warm energy that isn't solid. I hold its hands and follow.*
>
> *We're going toward a Milky Way, and we ride it. I'm going feet forward. On the sides are all these twinkling lights. The one that is like Tinker Bell is both masculine and feminine. She's taken me somewhere in a circle of light where we've stopped. It's beautiful, like a large round table of lights with other lights swirling in it.*

•••••••

I'd like the point out how, following Nathan's past life demise, his verbal description is entirely spontaneous and not something I prompt during the soul regression. Client regression elements are decidedly specific, and I look for them to support the knowledge I have gained over the years. As some would say, "You can't make this stuff up."

I can feel the vibration of the lights, but I don't yet know who they are. Tinker Bell says these souls that appear as lights want to see me. As they comfortably swirl around me, I know they're my friends. I can't put names on these fifteen or twenty souls. They welcome me back.

•••••••

This group of souls is my client's soul group, consisting of the souls he has known since the conception of his own soul. These are the souls with whom Nathan has spent the most time as HS, and also those who have been in his past lives. The spontaneity of soul regression is on full display as Tinker indicates that Nathan is not to stop and spend any amount of time with his soul group, indicating that critical guidance is about to surface.

Tinker is pulling me in a different direction. Here I go. There are tons of circles of light everywhere. They are groups just like my group. I wonder why Tinker pulled me out of my group. She tells me I have someplace else to be.

There's a more significant light ahead. I get closer and can see spokes from a darker middle. There's a group there that is not my friend group. This group is more powerful, and I'm in front of them. It's kind of like The Last Supper.

This group wants to say something to me. One in the middle is in charge. They seem to be whispering to each other. Tinker is there with me and wants me to wait. The one in the middle welcomed me back. I can't yet discern their comments. The coordinator laughed like I was supposed to know.

I feel the radiance of love from them with no judgment. Tinker holds my shoulder gently and asks me to take in the love from the council. It feels like there's too much to take in. Tinker says to take another breath. I am sitting while they stand. I feel connected to them somehow through this love.

•••••••

As in Madeline's regression content, the word *love* comes up repetitively in Nathan's content. As a regression therapist, I must consider unique aspects like keywords. To define love, we could use terms such as *devotion*, *tenderness*, *attachment*, and *passion*. But human language is inadequate when it comes to portraying the concept of higher love, or what our spiritual guides desire for us to embody and infuse on earth.

A client's HS and guide are distinctly aware of the opportunity during regression to download critical information and lead the client forward in deciphering who they are as a soul and why they are in body currently. Stay with me as we pay attention to what Nathan verbalizes, such as wings and love, which we understand are signs that he is an ARS. Even though for years I have witnessed paramount teachings received intuitively by my clients, I still need to be more immune to the power and essential nature of what arises.

> *One of the council members at the end of the table says that I worry too much. I always worry about how things are going to turn out. Tinker tells me again to be sure to remember the love. One of them reminds me that I'm always provided for.*
>
> *They emphasize remembering "who you are." They explain that I am divine. I have everything I need if I would use it. I am asked why I hold back when "you know what you need to do."*
>
> *This group would be my guidance counselors. They are the ones who asked me to incarnate. In my past life, I died young because I held back. In life today, I hold back from being more authentic.*

• • • • • • •

It is human to brood about the outcome of our decisions or having sufficient financial resources. Nathan's council member reminds him to operate less from his human fears and more from trust in his soul and support from his guides. When we function more from our heart and higher wisdom, we open the door to a vantage point that is less contaminated than the party line of the problematic world of humans.

Ask Yourself

How often do I resist following my intuition or my heart's desire? We often lean toward doing precisely what our guides and our HS want us to do. Our decisions must be based on both head and heart, with either capability alone being insufficient. That leap of faith may open a new door in our life.

Nathan's narrative continues below; look for what his guides mean by stating he is divine, as another likely puzzle piece is explained. One interpretation of the word *divine* is that we are all souls from the higher realm. At the same time, there is a strong probability that the guide's verbiage means more. Finally, note that these council members asked Nathan to incarnate again into his current embodiment. My mind and heart are always tantalized as I listen intently to a client's regression content, awaiting the meaning of what is said. A key component of guiding regression is that I must remain patient as the compelling revelations emerge.

> *Tinker is a spiritual guide for me and knows things I do not. She is my connection to the angelic realm. Tinker tells me I'm more than I think and encourages me not to think small. She explains that I have a greater power that I don't use. I've come into body in life today to remember that.*
>
> *My connection with the angelic realm has something to do with light. Tinker says I am a soul from the angelic realm. Now I feel like crying. Tinker and the council now ask Dr. Backman to help me remember who I am as a soul.*

• • • • • • •

Nathan finds out he is an ARS, with more extensive power than he expected. Souls from the angelic realm have wings, which supports my conclusion that Nathan originates from the celestial high-frequency dimension of wisdom that has many labels (God, Source, Great Spirit, Shechinah, and Manu). ARS are always guided by souls from the angelic realm, including the archangels.

History tells us that Leonardo da Vinci was either a homosexual or bisexual. For centuries, da Vinci, considered one of the greatest painters of all time, hid his private romantic relationships. As I facilitate a soul regression, my mandatory role is to weave a tapestry of understanding for my client's soul. At times, I will bring a client back for a follow-up regression. In Nathan's case, I was intuitively led to suspect that he was the soul of da Vinci in his first life, which surfaced in his soul regression. After delving back into regression with Nathan, it appeared highly likely that my hunch about da Vinci was valid. Experienced souls can continue to embody on earth to meet humanity's needs.

My repository of broad-ranging soul content is the litmus test I use silently as I take in what my client verbalizes. I have already absorbed the interview specifics of my client's life from birth. By combining the regression features, the interview, and my intuitive guidance, I discuss and support my client in determining the purposeful nature of the soul regression. Nathan's guides implored him to remember his soul nature and think big, knowing he is connected to the light, which translates as Source wisdom.

My council tells me that my struggle with weight is about past life and shows me the opposite. My weight is so I can experience fullness. They say it's about being fulfilled. I am using food to feel fulfilled. It's about delight and not about my weight. I can eat less and feel delight. I am being told that ARS in body need to eat less than other souls.

I am blocking prosperity. I need to surrender the way I think that prosperity should come. I'm told that I chose poverty in my childhood family so I would know the contrast. Also, talking to my guides does not feel mystical. This is not what I thought it would feel like. It simply feels natural. I am on the right track.

Should I include anything else? They say I'll know it when I see it. They seem like smart-asses. Then they tell me that I don't need to know ahead.

•••••••

Many of us struggle with issues tied to weight and body image in the human body. Past lives often play a crucial role in our concerns about our size. For example, I have a past life where I died from gluttony, and I have grappled in my current life with related eating habits. Nathan has a similar past-life remnant. So many souls in body have preplanned a challenge in life today to find satisfaction in life that is not quenched through how much we eat. Think about what creates delight outside of food and drink.

To express the impressive value of the deep-seated insights spoken by my clients in soul regression is challenging, at best. Never lost on me is the experience of witnessing the soul awareness each client gains. Nathan shared a pivotal detail about how his everyday dietary intake relates to being an ARS. With many clients, I have witnessed a guide's explanation that certain souls in body need to eat less than others. I invite you to talk to your body and guides about what would be *most* useful regarding what you eat and drink.

My team of guidance counselors are ARS. I ask why it is so hard at times. They say it's because of the human condition. It's as hard as you want it to be. Don't buy into it.

I had to wait until I was older for my soul group to be with me. The color that my soul emanates is blue. Also, they tell me that my father's alcoholism was divinely orchestrated. They tell me to ignore what people say, think, or do. They are present to help me grow.

•••••••

We round the corner of Nathan's soul regression to hear him talk about his support team of guidance counselors. No one incarnate is ever left without advice from a spiritual guide about living our present life. ARS are either guided by other ARS or by their own HS. Such critical statements of guidance are beneficial if, and only if, we are willing to respect and absorb them. Life in the human body includes human emotions that are not soul-level emotions. For example, concern is felt by souls, while intense fear stems from our human lives and personalities. One powerful teaching is that when we interpret the events of our human life as total roadblocks, this perspective arises from our human self, not our soul self.

Nathan's life script includes working through various steps before like-minded souls he has known from past lives show themselves. With intention, he was scheduled to trek through multiple issues before finding a comfortable bond with other folks. Blue is a high-frequency color that signifies evolutionary energy of approximately an eight on a ten-point scale. As a regression therapist, I pay attention to spoken details that fit a pattern of what I know to be true about ARS. Intelligent energy created to support the highest orchestration of earth that emanates from the divine realm is always equal to an eight or nine of soul evolution. Thus, we know that Nathan's soul color is consistent with being an ARS.

Consider people that are or have been part of your life. Who played a role in the growth-producing classroom for your benefit? Who has been your ardent sidekick from the get-go? Both are intentional in your walk through this life. You encounter the life you want based on your attitude, just as Nathan's guides tell him to ignore people's words and actions. Utilize your life experiences for your evolution and that of others around you.

In Summary

ARS are highly unique in their nature and approach to life. Please remember that you cannot be two different soul origins, such as both an ARS and an IPS, nor can you be an EBS and an IPS. An ARS illustrates an ongoing loving and accepting nature, which is somewhat difficult to put into words. Many, if not most, ARS are inextricably tied to the divine, perhaps from a religious context, although often not. Though all experienced souls are generally sensitive to energy and emotion, I suggest that an ARS is the *most* sensitive and caring type of person.

Things to Think About

- From innumerable soul regression clients, the angelic realm and the cadre of ARS come to the surface spontaneously in client regression descriptions.
- Love, compassion, peace, and truth are the hallmark energy of ARS.
- ARS have a loving soul essence core that is strong, unique, and deeply caring.

Homework to Determine if You Are an Angelic Realm Soul

1. Do you struggle often with humans being less than loving and compassionate? An ARS will often struggle at a level of eight on a ten-point scale.
2. How do you define divine energy, and have you felt a direct connection with divine energy or the archangels?
3. Does your life purpose align with compassionate energy for a specific person or group?

CHAPTER SEVEN

Benevolent and Omnipresent Spiritual Guides

> There is a deep need in the world just now for guidance—almost any sort of spiritual guidance.
>
> —CARL JUNG

Direction from a guide manifests in various ways. Let's say you are seeking a new job. The first three applications fail. The fourth application may be for a role you question if you're sufficiently qualified for but which strongly draws your attention. To your surprise, you are hired during the initial interview. Your guides have likely intervened to influence your hiring. Ask questions, and listen carefully to your intuition to determine if your primary guide is your HS or a separate soul. Trusting your instinctive ability, tap into whether your primary guide is an EBS, IPS, or ARS.

Omnipresent Spiritual Guides, Free Will, and Karma

Being assisted by a spirit guide is not a privilege; it's automatic, just as a baby has parents and a student has teachers. Our spirit guides support each moment of our lives. Trust that you are always guided, because you are.

As you travel the path of soul progress, the curtain opens to reveal the truth: your HS orchestrates each embodiment. Gradually scaling the rising and thorny details of each life, you serve two masters: the evolution of your soul and the evolution of the universe. Your original soul design, prebirth agreements, and potential addendums to heighten your evolution become obvious as life ensues. As a young soul, you find that initial learning is mainly self-serving; with ongoing soul accomplishment, the focus becomes a balance between your growth and that of others. Ultimately, the arrival station has a sign overhead that reads Giving Is Receiving.

Free will is a crucial component of whether we follow our higher guidance. Humans have the unique gift of being free, which can cut both ways. Our guide implores us to make the most functional and evolutionary choices. The intention to balance past-life karma is an element of most incarnations. Did you have a life where your choices were more self-absorbed, or did you live to bolster others? All of us have walked through a lifetime without a North Star, leading to decisions mostly beneficial for ourselves. No matter our guide's input, we can go against it. A better option is to act above and beyond our agreements, using free will to evolve more than was intended in one incarnation.

Higher Self or a Separate Soul as Your Spiritual Guide

We always have a primary or lead spiritual guide who is ever present. There's a catch in who our guide is, however, that is essential to realize. It is a misunderstanding to assume that your primary guide must be a soul separate from your own soul.

Often, a client describes the challenge and frustration of intuitively accessing their guide. Over many years with clients of each soul origin, I've discovered why IPS and ARS often do not believe they can sense their guide. EBS always have a primary guide who resides in the spiritual realm of earth. Usually, this primary guide is different from the soul of a loved one. Often, an EBS has a team of guides that may include loved ones, the HS, and other souls. Soul regression clients at times describe a council of experienced guides who are present to provide a route to follow. Arriving at a council meeting in the higher realm indicates to me that my client is likely an EBS.

Our primary spiritual guide is always more evolved than we are currently. Primary guides for IPS and ARS frequently differ from EBS. The HS acts as the guide for 60 to 70 percent of all non-EBS. The reason for being guided by your own soul is simple. When IPS and ARS agree to embody on earth, they are already advanced souls at a level of seven and higher on the ten-point scale of evolution. When your HS is sufficiently experienced, taking on the role of at least one of your guides is automatic. IPS and ARS most often have only one guide.

When clients arrive for their soul regression, I explain that a spiritual guide will make itself known during the regression. Often, my clients share that they are challenged, or it seems impossible, in everyday life to connect with a specific guide. Two likely explanations exist: either the client is an EBS and they sense a team of guides rather than one guide, or the client assumes their primary guide must be a soul that is not their HS. In either case, once the soul regression is complete, the client will know the identity of their guide.

Intuitive Communication with Your Primary Guide

To access your guides through intuition, practice and more practice becomes the key. Exercising your intuitive muscle is like using a cord pulley to open drapes to see through a window. Many years ago, my compulsion was to establish an intact spiritual practice every morning. I chose a specific time, set up a spiritual area in my home, and began my unwavering daily ritual of a shamanic drumming journey, leading me into relaxation and a state of intuitive reception. Remember that some of us gain intuitive detail through our mind's eye, emotional clues, physical sensation, or simply a knowing. Our intuitive skill is aligned with our nature of being primarily visual, emotional, body centered, or cognitive.

The upshot of my newly established routine was a deepening of my respect and acceptance about being a soul with spirit guides and intuition. I found myself more comfortable with my spiritual beliefs and equipped with greater trust in my instincts. As time passed, I became more aware of general guidance and guides.

As you exercise your intuitive capability, your trust will expand. Guidance is everywhere; you'll need to pay attention. In the early 1990s, much to my surprise, my spiritual awareness began to germinate. An example of my clairabilities came into sight as I drew open the draperies. Clairkinesthesia, or body sensation, showed up first. I noticed a sudden high-pitched sound or pressure change in one ear, signaling me to pay attention. Over time, my intuitive interpretation of my ear sensation increased, and I sensed a cognitive message from my guides. For example, if my husband suggested that I check on my elderly mother, my ear would ring as confirmation to make the call. The more I honored these ear symptoms, the more they happened—and the implication of each signal was often valid.

Guides appear in soul regressions often as energy, or with a description of a body. Descriptions of guides are as vast as the universe. A wise older man in a robe or a female with soft flowing garments is frequent imagery for guides. Guides often present their energy in literal form for individuals to sense. The characteristics of the guide's energy are likely translated into an image. An animal as a guide may carry meaning, such as a bear, indicating the person must embrace their power and strength. A raven generally indicates the mystical unseen world. It is also common for an IPS to have a guide from their home location. The physical structure of such beings is animallike, such as a mantis or it having a large head and lizardlike skin. Guides manifest through many images to provide specific details to people about their level of evolution and soul origin.

Prepping Our Soul to Become a Guide

Your agreement to evolve as a soul and support the evolution of humanity includes another critical intention. EBS evolve from lifetime to lifetime on earth, balancing karma and gaining dharma. IPS and ARS arrive on earth with a higher degree of evolution and continue to evolve through earth's lives. All souls agree that their HS, over time, will gain the skill to serve as a guide to incarnate souls on earth. Your soul may already function as a guide to one or more incarnate souls on earth. Becoming a guide is an honor and a key responsibility. At times in our everyday lives, we can feel the commitment and effort of supporting others.

Ask Yourself

When have you used your free will to make choices that resulted in expansion and greater fulfillment? What events in life today were prompted by your guide?

As you absorb Camilla's regression, look for indications of her soul origin, just as I do with each regression. Her deep emotional sensitivity to the inhumane treatment of others and related struggles is profoundly characteristic of an ARS.

CAMILLA: An Angelic Soul with Guidance

I'm outside at a war scene, and it's hot. I'm a muscular middle-aged man with sandals and armor, holding a circular shield. There's a lot of death, and I'm sad about so many bodies near me. I feel a global sadness for these people who have died, but I don't know any of them personally. It seems I was a leader who caused all this death because of my actions.

Now I'm old and in bed. Still, I'm so sad about the pain I caused others because of my actions. I deeply regret all my lives when I was affected by my position of power as a leader. I know it will take time to work out these actions of mine or my karma. My beloved wife is with me.

I've died and am moving away from the scene quickly. It's just peaceful now. I sense the light of God in front of me, with three guides to my left and Jesus to my right. They are simply with me but haven't communicated yet.

I'm told my journey is about the love of self and others. This space where I am is just pure love. I go to earth to learn and teach about love. Then I return from earth to the Source of love. I don't understand why all this makes me cry.

Divine energy tells me that I am now in the space and Source of love that I am to bring to earth. You are on earth to love fiercely, even in the slightest interaction with people. Most simply, you are to be loved on earth. It doesn't need to be grandiose.

The narrative I have of being a fuckup and that I don't belong in my life just doesn't exist in the space where I am as a soul now. You must overcome that to be more of a loving presence on this earth. You are to feel in a position of power that is quite simple. In life today, I am an extension of God. I am to love.

I sense that my soul has wings. The divine tells me that I am an ARS. I've had seventeen lives on earth. I'm told that my gifts are loving people with their beauty and ugliness. I have compassion for people's darkness. My primary guide is Jesus.

•••••••

The spontaneous evidence in this soul regression clearly indicates Camilla's origin as an ARS. Profound past-life regret surfaces in her life today, indicated by her struggle to find small and large ways to convince herself of her worthiness. As an ARS, it is easy to feel sizable emotional sensitivity.

I have a past life that is holding me back in life today. I was a dark-skinned woman during Jesus's life. I married for status and didn't marry my true love. I betrayed myself. I must learn to let that life go. Regardless of karma needing to be released, this is all part of being human. As an ARS, I came to earth to learn about being in an earth body. On earth, I am learning about human love, and not marrying the one I truly love must be let go.

I come to earth to partake in being human. As an earth being at this time, I've taken on the human narrative that I'm not supposed to be intimate with the one I genuinely love. That's not who I truly am as a soul who knows love.

My parents, on the other side, are human, messy, and beautiful. I'm grateful to have learned about love in this life with my parents. I am to know grief and love and loss and gratitude and compassion with my sorrow. It was all necessary.

When I have thoughts and feelings of anxiety and depression, I must remind myself these are all human symptoms. It's not who I am. I must lean into this space, more of the light that I am.

•••••••

Even though I witness client regression content multiple times most weeks, I have not become immune to the power of the revelation. Past-life elements can be almost inextricably embedded in our emotions and behavior unless we uncover and release trauma. Marrying for power versus love is inadvisable and unhealthy. An ARS is reactive to emotional aspects of life, usually more so than souls of earth and interplanetary origin.

Camilla has carried forward her past life pain by continuing to avoid honesty about who she loves. As she says, "I am a soul who knows love," which is not a superficial comment. Key emotions in the human world allow us to expand, not contract. As I have explained to many clients, we must express our genuine emotions without becoming mired in them.

I continue to sense the communication I'm receiving is coming from God. Jesus is an evolved soul who speaks to me through love and compassion. I feel that God speaks to me through Jesus, whose life of love and sacrifice was crucial.

I am to tune in to Jesus and the three guides in my everyday life. These guides are part of the angelic realm. But Jesus is not part of the angelic realm. I'm being told that the three guides speak to me through my intuition, even when I am not aware of the Source of my guidance. They assist me to intuit where to be in my life and to know my worth. They are a constant presence.

•••••••

Western religion based on Abraham is founded on accuracy and human interpretation. Our task is to do our best to separate what could be called the wheat from the chaff. Because ARS serve Source, guidance is often received directly. Jesus, known as Yeshua during his life, spread love and taught caring for others. Unfortunately, many humans weren't ready to absorb his perspective and human ego battles ensued. Two thousand years later, humanity continues a spiral of power and self-absorption. Please note that I am not advocating any religious belief; rather, we must honor all living things.

Camilla's soul regression unveils her ongoing intuitive development in life today. Current details of our value and path forward are available through instinct and trust. As I cross-reference the content of multiple clients, I know that the Yeshua soul is not a member of the angelic realm. Yeshua is an advanced EBS who works in conjunction with IPS and ARS to focus on humanity's needs. An ARS can have more than one guide, but the majority of ARS have only one guide, which is their HS.

IPS can arrive in a human life with intrusive energy, creating fear and emotional imbalance. Without an awareness of our soul design, misinterpretation and misdiagnosis can occur in our present life, leading to more significant trauma. Join me now with Hayley, another fascinating but at times challenged IPS with an Arcturian guide.

HAYLEY: Releasing Fear and Blame as an IPS with Arcturian Guidance

I am somewhere vibrant, beautiful, and bright. Then I get a dark image, like an old-world environment. It's balmy and fresh. I'm alone. There's a butterfly and a pool of water, with trees around it. My feet are bare, and my brown hair is extended to my waist.

My body feels ethereal and not solid where I am. I am sensing two contrasting worlds of peace, safety, and calm. When I'm there, I can get in touch with various beings who feel nontoxic. I'm with a being who has a body of pure golden light. They came to see me long ago when I was struggling in my life.

This golden being is with me now to help with my lifelong struggles. This is my interplanetary Arcturian guide from my home location in the celestial realm. I was told that I was needed on earth now and had been on earth before. My intentions for life today are related to the universal picture. There's a lot at stake. I feel the embrace of this golden being's protection and light. I'm struggling a bit because I've been impacted both as a soul and as a human by lower-level energies that seek to draw me offtrack.

•••••••

Vibrant, beautiful, and bright are vital aspects of Hayley's nontoxic home setting. The golden being who presents in her regression is familiar to her, having visited earlier in her life. Advanced souls, such as an IPS, always arrive in body to advance humanity and beyond. At the same time, unevolved souls can intrude into our human life to do their toxic work and delay the progress of our earthly culture. Emotional imbalance in life today may be reflective of these lower energies.

The souls like me are telepathic with healing energies. We come to earth to help with the universal picture of peace and beauty. Yet we are uncertain of earth's path in this bigger picture that is so needed. It is so easy for earth to fall to a lower frequency rather than to elevate. I do not know how to protect myself from the darker energy on earth.

The golden being tells me people have been sent to help me fend off negative energy. I must let myself be helped. Golden being says I am a unique soul. The pain on earth is tough for me. I can get trapped by negative energy that seeks to block earth's evolution. I am to be consciously always connected to the golden being.

Golden being takes me to a beautiful, vibrant, and safe setting in the celestial realm. Bright golden light is pouring down on me. I needed to go back to this place so that I feel protected.

I've been on earth numerous times. As a soul, my universal role reflected on earth is to unify all beings. My soul's work is like a compass to create a web of interconnection. My abilities are to provide energy to connect higher energetic planes to earth, leading to universal cohesion and earth's evolution. Some souls do not want this solidarity that raises the vibration of earth.

Golden being explains they do what they can to protect me from lower energy. I am to do my best to stay in situations with a higher vibration. This is big for the universe and the planet. My guide believes I don't realize the meaning and intensity of who I am and the energy I bring to the earth. I make it my fault when dark energy affects me.

• • • • • • •

Hayley brings deep intuitive abilities and healing capacity to her current life. To function with instinctive awareness of how to aid others, a person must be relatively porous energetically, which can lead to an impact from low-level, unhealthy forces. It is important not to live in fear but to be acutely aware of our emotions and instability that may not be our fault. Guidance and healthy support are always available if we trust and discern how to receive it.

My client is reminded of her beneficial home location to avoid becoming mired in energy seeking to pull her offtrack from her healing skills. Earth must elevate. For eons, earth has advanced, but not to the degree of peace and equality needed. Hayley is one of the souls who has agreed to function in a healing capacity. She must know herself as a soul and constantly be aligned with her golden being guide. The light always overcomes the dark. It is all too easy as a human to question and disconnect from our core experienced soul self and our life's intention today.

> *If I could grasp the potency of what I carry to earth and release the fear and self-blame, then the lower vibration would not as quickly take hold. I'm angry the lower energy got to me, and I feel I haven't succeeded. My job is to connect the highest universal energy to earth. These lower beings pull me away from my home vibration. I have chosen to come here. My home base is part of the bigger picture. I am very invested in supporting humanity's evolution.*
>
> *The romantic relationship I have today is with a soul from my home location. This is the first time we've known each other. Unfortunately, this soul tries to block my progress and intentions on earth. I allow this relationship to be disempowering. I can stop this unhealthy energy by fully stepping into my power and soul evolution. I must be in my expansive healthy energy from home.*

•••••••

Hayley's golden being guide must be heard, as it is a crucial component for her remaining emotionally balanced and on her path to bring light and a healthy perspective to those seeking her services as a healer. The more advanced we are as souls, the higher the vibration and perspective we offer humanity. Being caught in anger and diminishing ourselves for lack of accomplishment will lower our frequency. A surprising yet essential recognition Haley has is that she must end her romantic involvement, which is one of low energy that seeks to draw her offtrack.

Ask Yourself

What past-life memories have impacted your life, and what can you do now to let go? Have you been hard on yourself because you believe you've not accomplished your life intentions?

In a lifetime, we must learn to hold fast to honoring our true qualities as we make the most significant evolution. The challenge of being true to yourself demonstrates more soul experience and enables you to reach higher levels of advancement. When my regression client is not conventional, we discover the individual's experienced soul. Leena has several guides, which is indicative of being an EBS. Absorb the lesson that we must find time for play without constantly examining life from a profound perspective.

Loved ones who have passed already frequently meet us as we transition from a past life to bond once again with our HS. When healing from a past or current life is needed, my clients often will describe a spiritual hospital or cleansing center as the first step once a past life is discovered in the regression. Our guides meet our emotional, physical, and spiritual needs with nurturance.

IAN: Comfort from a Loved One After the Past Life

Dying is very easy. I am entering a hallway. There is someone there. He is there to let me know where I am and to refamiliarize me. I am in a half-circle hall with doors to different rooms. I feel comfortable. This is like a comforting white hospital without much detail.

Then I go up two marble steps to a room with a high ceiling and pillars. Now someone keeps popping up in front of me. He's trying to get my attention. He's dressed in a white Greek toga. It's my granddaddy. He gives me a big hug. I barely have the strength to hug back. Earth takes a lot out of you. His presence gives me strength. I feel a sense of relief as the anxiety I felt about decisions I made in my past life falls away. We welcome each other back here quite often. We've been a Source of strength for each other.

He wants me to relax in a courtyard with a beautiful garden. There's a fountain with grass, flowers, and foliage. This is a beautiful place to decompress. He stays with me to help me cope with my past life as a woman with little means and great physical demands. Granddaddy acknowledges the difficult decisions I had to make.

•••••••

Consider your granddaddy to be anyone who has transitioned to the other side and whom you trust unequivocally. For me, there was a woman, a close friend of my mother's, who served as that trusted nonjudgmental buttress to hear me and offer advice for my current life's path. She passed in my thirties. Energetically, there are spiritual comfort locations, such as water settings and gardens.

Assimilate Samantha's HS agreement to lay the groundwork for new souls to manage embodiment. For a soul to cope with immersion into the body and navigate an earthly life, extensive homework is required.

SAMANTHA: Meeting My Guide to Rejuvenate and Prepare Baby Souls

As I leave the past life behind, I'm just floating in a place with stars. I feel welcomed home, and there's no rush. Now I walk into a place resembling a cave with stalactites and stalagmites. I am moving toward a disk at the top of the stairs. Under the disk there is a crescent-shaped place where I lie down. The disk holds greater consciousness. As I lie under the disk, I am healed and rejuvenated. I feel held and enveloped in love. Then I see my guide, Rakesh.

Rakesh tells me I can go to this place to receive energetic caretaking anytime because my cells hold it in memory. I get up and move down a pathway with white pillars on either side. Now I see small bits of consciousness. These are like seeds that need to be nurtured.

These are baby souls fresh from the Source. They are gradually being prepared to incarnate. I help these young souls rest until they generate enough power to incarnate. These young souls of primordial material develop over time to gain self-awareness and expansion sufficient to begin their journey into embodiment.

•••••••

Rakesh underscores the higher consciousness of Samantha's place in spirit. At any moment in time, she can lie in or immerse herself in her crescent space. As a longtime nurse-midwife, Samantha comprehends her role with baby souls. Life in the body requires preparation as these seeds of consciousness gradually swell into capability for the challenges of incarnation. One of Samantha's roles is to aid these youngsters energetically.

Remember that your guide is always a more experienced soul than you. As a young soul, our guide may be significantly more evolved. Once we attain a degree of soul wisdom well beyond the average, our guide is like the university professor whose students are PhD candidates. As you absorb these particulars, remember that we all have a guide, sometimes more than one; at times, our primary guide is our HS. The greater our soul experience, the more our HS assists us, with or without another guide. In the following regression narrative, Gilda demonstrates how a sea change can happen and a new guide replaces your prior guide.

GILDA: A Changing of the Guard with My Guide

Following my passing during the French Revolution, I come upon a guide who is not my usual main guide. I don't recognize this guide, who tells me to call him teacher. At first I feel adrift without the calming familiarity of Paul, whom I have known as my long-standing guide. Teacher explains that Paul's soul-level obligations have shifted, combined with my decisions to widen the scope of my work in the human world. Teacher is one of the souls who coordinates the earthly spiritual realm. He explains that in my recent past lives, I have demonstrated a willingness to stand up for human behavior that I believe is right and just. Teacher has taken me on as his mentee because both of us are devoted to broad alterations of humanity.

My HS has recently been called to serve on the earth high council, which reflects my human shift as I offer support to people wanting to enhance their transformative ideas in various walks of life. Teacher commends me for being courageous and stepping more out of the box of what many believe are the limits and conventionality of my profession. Next, teacher explains that another evolved soul in the higher realm will become my secondary guide, which gives me the energetic support of both astute souls.

•••••••

Gilda's regression indicates critical points. Our primary guide can change within our present incarnation. Also, when we take the risk to redesign our lives and work in ways that are not the norm but are needed in human society, we impact the expansion of the role of our HS. As we reach a more elevated degree of soul evolution, we are often supported and mentored by two sagacious souls with broad incarnate experience. With more significant tasks as a human and a soul, it is not what we might call a picnic. We likely feel and note the alteration in our human life, which puts more pressure on us to step up. Often we must learn to cope with intensified energy that can affect our sleep, our body, and our relationships.

Teresa is a dear friend and colleague with conscious access to her past lives. As an Egyptologist, she keenly remembers the interplanetary guidance and intention of earth's earliest advanced civilization, which aimed to lead humanity to a place of peace and honor for all living things. When we grasp the original intent of our earth community to accomplish wholesome actions where everyone's needs are met, then every day our behavior reflects what the ancients desired.

TERESA: An Interplanetary Soul with Ancient Egyptian Lives

As a child of the seventies and eighties, I played on the ancient lands of Hadrian's Wall living in Northumberland, England. I ran through the countryside, seeing the spirit guardians of the ancient lands. My parents traveled with me to power sites and sacred lands. I had many unusual metaphysical experiences. I spoke with and received counsel from my spiri-

tual guides on all life matters, including my future service to humanity. My spirit guides always materialized in front of me.

As a child, I was spiritually wide awake, operating on a high-sensitivity spectrum that detected advanced beings and spirit. These guardians were my universal teachers. I learned how to magnetize light for healing and shielding. I learned how to read psychology and time. My earliest preschool memory is, "Why are these adults asking me to make purposeless petrol station pumps from washing-up liquid bottles?" I had many time travel experiences during childhood that shocked my conventional parents.

I spent my childhood questioning and experiencing spirit, consciousness, and reality. As a preschool child, I knew how to meditate, activate higher consciousness, and interact with light beings; I had knowledge and the capability of advanced technologies and guardians who traveled with me over incarnations. I was also exceptional academically.

At seventeen, I was my grandmother's gatekeeper upon her death. I had dreamed the details of her death six weeks previously. My psi abilities were blown wide open, and I began formal training in metaphysics in London. This would be my destiny.

I now live in Egypt on the same ancient gateways I inhabited in ancient times. I am an incarnation of the soul of Queen Nefertari, high priestess. I am Mery Re, high priest of Akhenaton and Tutankhamun and the last Nubian pharaoh of Egypt, Taharka. The ancient monuments activate and increase my abilities and ancient and future memories. I build new knowledge as a spiritual teacher and guardian of progressive psychology and new humanity. At the gateway of the great pyramids, Pharaoh Kafre materializes with winds through his valley temple to initiate the level of intelligence of this ancient and future civilization. I have a unique capacity to analyze and alchemize consciousness and history and predict intelligent futures. This destiny is witnessed, progressed, and protected in my terrestrial and extraterrestrial soul contracts. I believe new psychologies and timelines are being built across time and space within our universe, across civilizations. This is an imperative interaction for peace on earth beyond wars.

•••••••

IPS tend to be unique people with personalized attitudes, skills, knowledge, and way of life. Teresa is no exception and may even be more noteworthy than many IPS. Frequently she speaks of detrimental human life in the matrix, referring to living day-to-day with a self-centered materialistic focus. Teresa's primary guide, her HS, directs her to teach and function from a peaceful and universal caring mentality.

Liam unveils a regression that is typical of an IPS with substantial physical obstacles. For years, Liam, a man in his forties, has suffered from Crohn's disease and lupus, both considered autoimmune disorders, in which the immune system mistakenly attacks and destroys healthy tissue. Based on his experience, autoimmune disorders seem to occur in people who block their emotions and often are IPS.

LIAM: Not from Earth and Struggling to Live Within My Body

I'm in my mother's womb not long before birth. I have a strong sense of purpose for my upcoming life. It's been difficult to attach as a soul; it was hard to get through and come into body on earth. I've not been incarnated on earth many times. It's always confusing for me to work with this type of brain.

Now I'm in a past life. There's a barn and a house where someone lives. I am there too. I'm a freckle-faced child with red hair in braids. I'm wearing a cotton gown that ties at the neck. I have some teeth missing. The man here is a healer; he has me helping him with his work. One of his goats is ill, and he must kill it. He has me hold the goat down; I'm not scared to do this.

There's nothing to be afraid of when he must take the life of an animal. He shows me how to see the animal's spirit leave its body. He cuts the goat's throat. Both of us feel a whirlwind come out of the goat. The goat was very ill. We thank the goat's spirit for being with us.

This man I am with is essential to me. His eyes are intense. He's been my teacher. He found me wandering in the forest when I was ten years old.

It's later, and I am in my early thirties. The man has died. I live alone with many animals. The people in the village nearby are afraid of me;

they want to kill me. I'm so worried about the animals. Who will care for them? I release the healthy animals. I kill the ones that are old and tell their souls to go.

I feel bad for the animals. They each had a purpose for being my family. These other people do not understand. A group of men come to get me. I won't follow their ways or call on their type of God. They take me to the river and put a sack over my head. They put a rope around my feet and attach a rock. They dump me in the river, and I sink to the bottom. My soul exits from the center of my chest.

Immediately my guide, Brooke, is here with me. She reminds me that she shows up in my life as a crow. I'm told that I did the right thing in the past life. My purpose in life today is to teach that spirit is everywhere. The density of my body on earth is not my normal. This causes many of my physical anomalies.

There is more than one reason I've had so many physical issues in my current life. My home base in spirit is different from earth. The beings where I come from want to understand the illness of the human body, so I am to bring back information about physical pain to my home base. This information can help others from home come to earth and be able to cope with the human body. What is essential is that the physical issues do not keep us from separating from the spirit. They tell me that the physical complications I have are not who I am.

They ask me to sit in a beautiful meadow and healing energy pulses through my body. I feel a warm golden light moving through me. Then I'm taken to be with all the animals I killed in the past life. All these animals greet me. They understand unconditional love. The soul of an animal is lighter than a soul that incarnates in a human body. Animals come to the plane where I live now to help humanity.

I am told to speak and live my truth, trust in myself, and always ask for guidance when needed. The diseases I have as a human being help others who are incarnate understand how to cope with physical pain. As a soul, I agreed to bring this understanding. I am to help incarnate healthcare professionals develop new treatments. When I have a physician who doesn't seem to respect me for who I am, I am to think kinder thoughts. I am to do more healing on myself.

•••••••

In today's life, Liam is deeply attached to animals and nature, particularly trees that give voice. As an IPS, he brings excellent gifts to earth to assist many; he must honor who he is at the core. Brooke, Liam's guide, automatically offers clarity about Liam as a soul. IPS are often unique in their style of dress and hairstyle. As an outside observer, you can speculate that an individual with a distinctive and colorful appearance who seems wise and spiritual is likely an IPS. Liam teaches practitioners who may inaccurately judge his visual appearance or knowledge as strange.

In Summary

A mentor and a confidante are words that best define the role of our primary spiritual guide. Conscious communication is ours for the asking when we trust our guide's omnipresence and unbridled support. Whether we are conscious through intuitions of our guide's direction or pay close attention to life circumstances and notice what arises and what doesn't, we are never left unaccompanied. If you think or know you are an EBS, seek direction from an evolved senior teacher, your guide. When you know or suspect you are an IPS or ARS, tap in intuitively to hear your HS and ask, "Are you my guide, or is another soul my guide?" Trust is essential to discover and communicate with your closest companion, your guide.

Things to Think About

- Keep a journal with a list of life decisions prompted by your guide.
- Explain in your journal why you believe your primary guide is or is not your HS.
- Consider the image and energy of your guide as an EBS, IPS, or ARS.

Homework to Discover Your Guide

1. When do you ignore the advice of your guide, and why?
2. In life today, are you preparing to serve as a guide?
3. Do you use images, emotions, body sensations, or knowing to hear your guide?

CHAPTER EIGHT

Your Immortal Loved One Across the Veil

> Grief is not a disorder, a disease or a sign of weakness. It is an emotional, physical and spiritual necessity, the price you pay for love. The only cure for grief is to grieve.
>
> —DR. EARL GROLLMAN

Losing a loved one, a relationship, an expectation, or anything we deeply care about serves our human and soul evolution. Loss is inevitable. Permanent trauma is not. Often, the sign of a loved one's presence on the other side is ignored either because we do not know what to look for or we disbelieve. When we face the passing of people familiar to us in our past lives, our emotions may be heightened.

Loss and Grief: In Service to Our Soul Evolution

One of life's greatest heartbreaks is the passing of a loved one. Years ago, following the premature birth and transition of our second child, I found myself in a typical deeply painful grief process. It was as if I had the emotional flu with no understanding of how grief affects us. How to cope with the emotions of loss was a mystery. Nor did I realize that the acute suffering would not last forever.

Over time, my picture of how to mourn shifted into clarity. Navigating the mission of loss must have two perspectives. For one, the experience of having a beloved someone die is gut-wrenching, resulting in emotions that require attention and expression. Essential support people must offer you a constant dose of acceptance, lack of judgment, and off-the-chart caring.

At the same time, it is a crazy balance of allowing you to emote on and on, almost to a fault if that's possible. In the mix must be people who nearly force you to get out of the house for a walk, a meal, or just a look at the sunrise and sunset. Grief likely will not 100 percent go away but will soften and become less frequent. How deeply you love what you have lost equals the degree of pain you experience. Acute grief is never over in six weeks or even six months. Do not absorb someone else's need for you to feel better if that's not you now. Accept all your feelings, from all-encompassing sadness to intense anger.

In combination with the expression of emotion surrounding grief is the core truth that when we transition out of the body, the portion of our soul energy that caused us to live and breathe returns to our HS. Relatedly, the soul energy of your mother, aunt, friend, child, or anyone else remains a constant. Whether you find pennies in odd places or hear your loved one talking to you in your head, the soul is immortal. Trust that only the physical container called the body departs. Simply put, the essential components in your grief process are to feel and to trust. No feeling is right or wrong; it is a feeling, pure and simple. Trust you do have access to your loved one by knowing that intuitive communication is a two-way street, even years after physical death.

Loss is loss. By this I mean that a normal grief response is also tied to other key aspects of endings in your life. Have you had a pet die? Or has there been an alteration in your physical or mental capability? Did a job of yours come to an end? Even a divorce or the conclusion of a romantic relationship you'd grown beyond can bring forth emotions of grief.

Imagine music playing from the headphones you're wearing. "Over the Rainbow" from *The Wizard of Oz* is playing about a "land up high." The higher realm or spiritual realm where the souls of our loved ones reside as soul energy is a frequency. Remember that if you are an EBS, your soul is in the spiritual realm and tied to earth. If you are an IPS or ARS, your HS is in the celestial realm at your home base. As an IPS or ARS, you may have experienced a few encounters with grief and loss, either on earth or at your home location, leading to more significant challenges. The energy of the vast celestial realm is as real as your hand you can see. Also, the records of all your past lives exist at the frequency of the higher realm.

Prepare yourself to take in the following soul regression narratives as different clients share their discovery of past lives and who they are as a soul. When you know yourself as a soul, grief and loss hold wisdom and the conscious acceptance that a loved one goes on. Think about the song from *Titanic*: "My Heart Will Go On." The heart, meaning the soul, absolutely continues.

Sasha, a woman in her sixties, agonizingly faced the transition of her young adult son in a devastating car accident. Imagine yourself in the shoes of my client, an ARS filled with devotion and caring for others and focused on what is right and just. As Sasha, you carry the trauma of death and war, along with facing the inexplicable shock of losing your child.

SASHA: Angelic Soul Coping with the Loss of a Son

I'm in a kitchen with my mom. My feet are bare, and I wear a white shirt and shorts. I'm dirty. I want to help my mom, but I'm only about two years old. My hair is sandy brown, and I have blue eyes with puffy cheeks. I'm drooling because I'm still getting some of my teeth. I'm a little boy standing near a door.

It's later, and I'm a teen outside on a farm. There's a swing in a big tree. I have blue jeans and a T-shirt with darker hair and sticky stuff in my hair to keep it in place. I'm tall and handsome with a nice smile. There's somebody nearby.

Even though I should be doing my work, I'm talking to a girl. I like her a lot. She has on some school uniform. I know her well, and we're laughing. I feel peaceful. I can sense the wind blowing.

Now I'm twenty years old and wear a green uniform. I have shiny shoes and am walking on a dirt road with them getting dirty. I've come home for a short visit. I left the girl. I'm a soldier now.

I'm not near home now. I feel sad because I had to leave home. I wish I was still on my farm. I'm running, and my boots are heavy. I'm near farms and trees. It's loud in the distance but quiet where I am. I'm looking for someone. It's dangerous where I am. I'm a soldier, and I need help.

I'm so cold and scared of getting killed. I'm looking for a marker of some sort. I feel that I was dropped from the sky here as I parachuted to where I am now. First I was all tangled. Now I'm running, and it's getting light.

I get to the marker and go into a gate. I'm still so cold. I see another soldier. I'm close to where I'm supposed to be. I see people I know. We're moving along a wall as a group of soldiers. There's water that we're walking through. I am so cold.

• • • • • • •

In this past life, Sasha was male and served as a paratrooper, likely in World War II, who parachuted into a military operation. As a soldier, Sasha struggled with leaving the family farm and coping with active duty, which was frightening and cold. My client is a determined personality who agonizes over numerous aspects of human life that are not her choosing.

I'm in an old airplane hangar by myself. I'm about fifty years old. I have gray hair now. I'm remembering what happened and how it changed me. The war still affects me. There's this corner of darkness inside me from the death, destruction, and loss. This old hangar is in a field where I feel comfort because it's safe here to remember my pain. I feel tears now.

I'm smoking a cigarette. My hair is always a mess, but I'm still handsome. It reminds me of being a boy with my hair always hanging in my face. Many either died in the war or didn't survive long after the war. I don't feel lucky or privileged.

I feel it was my destiny to be able to come home from the war. Yet I feel confused and disappointed about being left by the others, being the one who understands the trauma of war and loss. I don't ever want to see it again.

I am making a pact that if I allow myself to remember, then I will always seek peace. I'm a good person. I have a family and have done right even though the war caused me to feel tortured inside.

• • • • • • •

Sasha lays bare the nearly permanent agony of war that affects the man she was, his fear of remembering alongside his purposeful commitment to never forget the senseless acts of war. As a soul, Sasha pledges to seek peace no matter what happens. What could be more crucial to our human culture than negotiating and balancing all people's needs? My client also realizes that emotional pain must stimulate soul evolution, leading to acceptance of loss. Further, Sasha is a psychotherapist in life today, aiding others' resolution and solace.

Now it's the end of my life. I've had a good life. There's a funeral at a beautiful wooden church, perhaps built in the early 1900s. There are two of me. It is my funeral. There's this very old, stooped-over man watching the funeral. It's okay that I have died. People who care and know I was a good person have come to the funeral. I died at eighty-two years old. There's also a girl in the swing outside the church.

I'm traveling now away from that past life. I'm in a quiet place in space. There are twinkling blue lights. There are two guides here, one male and one female. The female guide agrees that the male guide will talk first. I'm told I don't take enough time to be quiet and hear my guides. But I'm told that I listen to him more often than her. They know I'm mad about my son dying, so I let myself get lost in the noise.

To do what I came to do I must be more still. They hear me when I communicate in the blue skies. We made a pact in the blue skies. My son, who is on the other side, my husband, and I made a pact in the blue skies. I do not remember that pact we made in the higher realm.

•••••••

Sasha's life as the soldier who survived WWII ends as her HS can both observe the funeral from above as well as sense being the older man present at his own service. Past-life regression research indicates that many souls alive during WWII either reincarnated quickly or had incarnations that overlapped in time. Our soul has the energetic ability to multilocate. Thus, Sasha absorbs more than one vantage point to broaden the value of her past-life and soul discovery. The girl in the swing is a reminder to not forget about love. Blue energy indicates the evolved energy where Sasha's guides reside and the higher realm where her son's soul exists. Sasha lets distractions create noise in her life to block her awareness of guides and her son. Not getting lost in life's fullness is a key component to evolving. At the soul level, Sasha, her husband, and her son come to an agreement that becomes clearer as the regression proceeds.

> *I resist pain. I see myself running outside with part mountains and part desert. My son cloud surfs with me. I can jump to a cloud where he and I can talk. Just below his cloud there's a park where I find my son. My male guide tells me there's a message for me if I take time to cloud surf.*
>
> *This guide is big and strong with long blond hair. My female guide says I keep myself distracted so I don't hear her. She tells me I can't take on the pain and suffering that happens to everyone, not just me. I take on the suffering of humans, animals, and plants.*
>
> *I am told that my expanded sensitivity to the suffering of all living things is due to my soul not having been on earth many times and originating in the greater celestial realm. My husband is an EBS. My son who passed some years ago is like me, a soul with few earth incarnations.*

•••••••

Taking time to tap into our intuition is key to receiving guidance from guides and loved ones. As Sasha allows herself to commune with her son and uses imagery, moving from cloud to cloud, she indicates openness to receive direction and love. The female guide illustrates how Sasha is overwhelmed by the trauma she senses from all living things on earth. This is a clue to Sasha's soul origin, as she learns her immediate family is a mixture of soul types. Sasha, an ARS, her son, an IPS, and her husband, an EBS, agreed to arrive on earth and work together to meld themselves as three different types of souls.

> *I want to know if I'm on my path. My intuitive image is of myself with hiking gear, a backpack, and an actual monkey on my back. My path is not straight, including highs and lows. Gabriel is a name that is important to me. I can hold a mirror, looking at myself, and he's in the reflection.*

My guides tell me that I have wings I can feel. But I'm detached from the wings because I am walking my path with the monkey. I am an ARS. I deeply respect IPS. Love and compassion show themselves in my life through chaos. I do not discern the essential pieces from the unimportant. I've lost sight of something I should know. I feel I'm spinning in my life. I am to calm the spinning.

My son tries to talk to me, but I can't always hear him because I am spinning. I feel emotive too often. I need to let go and go into quieter consciousness states. My angelic guide's name is Jonathan.

I feel connected to my soul when I sing and play my guitar. When I'm not congruent in my relationships, I lose the connection. Often, I'm not attached to my soul self. When I'm connected, I'm tied to beauty, the Source, and a river of power that energizes me.

I must remove the monkey from my back. I've been too close to the darkness. I am a being of light and must stay close to the river of power. When I'm near the dark, I cannot find my way. I'm not a being who can be messing with the dark.

•••••••

The metaphor of hiking gear indicates Sasha's intention to set a path to higher evolution. A contradictory metaphor is the monkey who must be let go. No one's path is straight. Plus, when the name Gabriel emerges in regression, I make a note that potentially my client is an ARS.

Sasha's advisers reveal she is an ARS, but she blocks herself from this powerful, compassionate energy. By allowing chaos and emotional distress into her life, she resists embracing her core tender energy. Sasha battles with her life circumstances, which lead to constant reeling with pain and stress. Music is an avenue to the depth of her soul origin of heart-centered mercy.

Sasha must take time to quiet and tap in intuitively to her HS. A profoundly important message for all of us, including Sasha, is to step away from diabolical energy and attach to the river of light and truth. ARS are of the highest vibration. Delving into low vibration will trigger suffering and hamper letting her light shine.

Ask Yourself

What was the first critical loss in your life? How did you cope with this first loss, and how did it help you grow? Who was your support during your first loss? Loss is inevitable. How we cope with loss expands our mental, emotional, and spiritual strength. In grief, we can block our emotions, disallowing intuition to work for us.

Outdated Social Customs Coupled with Past and Current Child Loss

Surviving the passing of a child in both past and current life may seem monumentally tricky and more than anyone would need to bear. Oftentimes, the more onerous the life events on the surface, the more likely we've agreed to climb higher rungs of the evolutionary ladder. Kacey and her husband faced the loss of their year-old son from Sudden Unexplained Death in Childhood. On a typical workday, months before their child's passing, Kacey had dropped her two children at daycare. As she arrived at work, she was struck with abdominal pain and heard in her head, "One of your children will die." Kacey did her best to dismiss this frightening message.

KACEY: Feeling Grief or Numbing Grief

I see my hand with polished nails, and I have white skin. I have a big dress and a hoop skirt. It's awful because I can't sit down. I'm outside on cobblestones. I see a horse and a carriage.

There's a coach with a man and a top hat. I get into the carriage with him because I must do this. It's predetermined. I feel despondent. It's done. Now I am going away with him. I can't change it. I have no voice. I must marry someone I do not love and did not choose.

It's later. I'm outside with my children, and they're playing. I have two boys; one is blond, and the other is brunette. I love them so much. This is not a glamorous life. I don't have fancy nails and hair anymore. I am so proud of my boys.

One of my boys has died. It was an accident. They were just playing. I'm trying to get him out of the water. I think one of my sons drowned in the water. I don't know what to do. I'm so alone. My other son is with me. But my husband is gone.

There's no one to help. I am so angry with everything and everyone. They made me come here. I didn't have a voice. If I hadn't come here, this would have never happened. I must bury my son in our yard. I am covering my son's body with dirt. There was nowhere else to bury my son. My husband is not coming back. I'm all alone, just me and my boy.

•••••••

In Western European culture, obligatory marriages, arranged by the male parent, were common until the late 1700s. Women did not have a voice and often were forced to marry for the sake of their family gaining more land or sharing power with another family. Kacey's past life seems to fit this antiquated social norm. Though her marital relationship seems distant, this past life reveals Kacey's love for her boys. She blames her life situation on having to marry someone who isn't a supportive spouse. With extreme pain, Kacey must face the accidental death of her child.

I start drinking because I'm so unhappy and angry. My drinking gets worse. My boy grows up and leaves. I'm not a good mother and not available. Now I'm old and alone. I'm just rocking on a porch and crying.

I want to take my life. I get so drunk. I shoot myself. Now I realize I'm still alive. The bullet missed, and it didn't work. I am mad, sad, and glad. I'm so confused. I can't even take my life. Nothing goes right in my life.

Now it is the last day of my life. I'm outside in the grass, and I'm very old. I am no longer angry. I forgave myself for everything. I had the choice to live or not. I chose to live. I can smell the flowers and enjoy the sun. I enjoy being by myself. I am grateful for my life. I just lie down, and I die.

I could have done my life better. I had hard lessons to learn. But I didn't die angry. I wish I'd been more available to my son, the blond-haired son who didn't die. My daughter of today is the soul of my blond son. I'm allowed to have a do-over with my daughter.

After my child died in life today, I started drinking, like in my past life. But I realized that if I kept drinking, I would waste my present life. So I chose to stop drinking and to live a healthy life. My guide comes forward. He tells me that I am at risk of making poor choices, like drinking too much. I must stop hurting myself.

•••••••

In her past life, Kacey gives up after her son dies. Alcohol is the numbing tool she uses to avoid facing her emotions. As well as not allowing her grief to flow and soften over time, Kacey is unavailable to her remaining son. Perhaps as intended by her spiritual guides, she is unsuccessful in ending her life.

Over time, Kacey rights her life by comprehending that her anger is destructive. Choosing to live rather than exist is the doorway to forgiveness. Determining how to approach our lives, no matter the traumas we've endured, is up to us. Choose gratitude. Please appreciate the beauty of how our lives are linked, knowing that the blond son's soul returned to Kacey as her beloved daughter.

Soul evolution is winding and sinuous, meaning that as we climb the rungs of experience, our guides become more exacting. Kacey must demonstrate to her guides and HS that she has the grit in her current life to avoid long-term depression and addiction. Two actions balance karma associated with self-harm: Upon completing an incarnation, we meet with our senior guides, who expect us, as a soul, to be honest about what we accomplished and what we would change in our recently completed life. In addition, we are to demonstrate behavior opposite to past harm in our upcoming lives.

As I leave that past life behind, I feel intelligent energy in the distance. Someone is coming now. I can feel them but cannot see them. Now I sense their energy enveloping mine. They are very powerful but hard to describe. I can see five lights in a half circle in front of me. This is my guidance team. I float with the five lights.

I'm told that I don't trust enough. My thinking is getting in the way. Now there's a plant with grass around it. I sit on the grass and feel more comfortable sharing candidly with my support team. My son, who passed, is with me now. He's in his little child's body like when he passed. He hugs me and tells me that if I listen, I can hear him. Again, he reminds me that he's always around, but I don't trust that I hear him. He tells me that I'm doing okay and doing a good job.

Now he takes me by the hand. We walk toward a white building. There is a square table with five lights around it. These are my team of guides. The coordinator of these guides is known as Ono. I hear my son and Ono regularly. Ono guides me in this life so I don't back out of my intentions. I'm to write down what I receive. When direction comes from my guides, I feel it more than I realize. I must trust what I feel because I function on emotion.

My guides are seated around a table like a half-moon. Nobody has a face, but I can feel they're all nice. I am an EBS. My life purpose is to move people forward. I'm to listen to my intuition and assist humans to grow. I hear my guide all the time, but I don't rely on this. I'm to write what I hear. The record of what I hear will help me believe. They are clear with me that I know how to help. I am not to worry about anything, including money.

There's no need to rush into my soul agreements. I'm still learning, and more will be revealed. I must learn to listen. Last, they insist I must stop drinking, which causes distortions. I must listen.

•••••••

Kacey's regression shows how we are always met and escorted as we traverse the veil with a past life in our rearview mirror. Our benevolent yet serious guides await the return of our soul aspect embodied in the completed life. Immediately, the soul of Kacey's son, who passed in this current life, steps in with love and reassurance. To reiterate, our body is dispensable, yet our soul endures.

Ono, Kacey's guide, is ever present as a powerful underpinning to her life intentions. Our guide communicates through intuitive imagery, emotion, body sensation, and simply knowing. Trust must be ongoing to receive our direction.

As an EBS, Kacey teaches others how to take to heart what we deeply believe are our life commitments. Spiritual people often question what they sense is their life mission because they know they are different from many others. As Kacey's guide tells her, "Learn to listen."

When a beloved spouse passes, we often feel alone and fear not knowing how to cope. For many, the surprise is that once we allow our deep grief to be in process, we arrive at a new place of peace. Frequently, what unfolds is meeting someone new, with the discovery that we can be fulfilled again in a relationship. Meet my client Madeline next, whose regression illustrates that all is not lost when a loved one transitions.

MADELINE: Grief, Karma, and Soul Expansion

Madeline is a woman in her sixties whose husband had recently died after a fifteen-month illness. He was described as a knowledgeable professional man who misused addictive substances and was prone to anger and anxiety. Though Madeline's marriage was difficult, she had a deep love and bond with her husband.

Following her husband's death, Madeline became reacquainted with a former love relationship that had been on hiatus for twenty-five years. She arrived for her between-lives soul regression to fully understand her relationship with her husband (James) and her newfound partner (Carlson).

I meet with my spirit guide, Omega. He welcomes me back into the spiritual realm. I am told that Carlson keeps me from sliding back into my pain. He is a safety net. Now I see Carlson. He is warm, supportive, a special companion, and less serious than I am.

I tell Omega that what has hurt me the most in my current life is my unfulfilled potential for love with my deceased husband. I am told that James was embodied as a test for him to experience love. He was being tested and refined. He had a great brain and much insight. He could have become godlike. Finding me was a gift because I softened his difficulty.

James was blocked from moving forward with his learning because of his addictions. In the future, he will have significant responsibility. He does know that I loved him. James comes forward to express his gratitude to me. "You did help me," he says. "It was beyond your control to change me. I had to live my life as I did." We go to a special place now where we can touch.

I am told that it is possible to love more than one person. With Carlson, I feel accepted. I am told to go play with him and have a good time. This may be a short or a longer relationship.

I will be with Carlson or someone else. I am to enjoy Carlson for now. We are very parallel, whereas James is on a different plane. He is a soul on a mission and has moved to a higher level. He is being prepared to be a strong leader. In his recent life, he has not been able to coordinate well. His threads were sticking.

I have known James and Carlson before. James is a vibrant and experienced soul. Carlson is joyful. He has intense passion and desire. "Always nurture the friendship with Carlson," I hear. "Be patient with him. Do not try to possess or control him. You are a gift to one another. Be gentle with yourself and others. Never hold back on loving and being loved."

•••••••

Madeline received a powerful clarification about the vital role she played in being married to James. Her spiritual team validates the depth of caring she offered him. They tell her it is now time for her to enjoy the calm beauty of her relationship with Carlson as a special, more compatible, and equal companion. The underlying message is that by demonstrating true love to James, Madeline gained the reward of an easy relationship with Carlson. Life's experience serves us in one manner or another; nothing is without purpose.

Imagine Sarah, with your intuitive eyes, who has fluffy, light-colored hair and a warmth that exudes from every pore. A few years ago, following the sudden passing of her beloved husband, she forced herself to live life while missing him immensely nearly every moment. Friends and acquaintances describe Sarah and her life partner as an example of what deep love, respect, and joy can look like.

Ask Yourself

How have I managed any losses in my life thus far? Have I allowed my emotions to be present? Have I reached out for support? Do I trust that if I dig into my feelings of grief I will come out the other side as a stronger person who believes in myself? Does my soul origin affect how I grieve?

SARAH: Angelic Souls as Life Partners and Grief

I'm in an iridescent white-light tunnel that is smooth like glass. As I exit the tunnel, I am surrounded by bright white light. The temperature is perfect, and I feel good to be here. I hear a soft, gentle humming. I am alone, but I don't feel alone. I know others are around. I am safe and comfortable. I am wearing a white gauzy gown. Yet I feel I am floating with a spotlight on me.

I'm unsure if I've been here before, but it is very comfortable. I'm so glad to be in this space. I'm big. It isn't easy to describe my size as I seem to be everywhere all at once. It feels lovely, so light and genuinely free.

I'm huge, and my face and hands are different in a way I cannot describe. The lower half of my body feels as if it is one, not two legs. I don't seem to have feet. Yet I can move around and float. Everything here is also big. I feel pleased and content. There's a buzz in the air and white light everywhere.

I sense other souls are nearby but have not said anything yet. I know this is the soul realm. Someone is coming. This is my spiritual guide. I feel the energy change, and the light is even brighter. My guide says I'm to call him Helper because that is what he offers me.

Helper shows me many people and tells me these are people on earth. He explains that where I am in this pure white light is the level of Source that guides humanity. I'm told that my HS resides at this level. My role in life is to aid humanity because I come from Source.

• • • • • • •

When Sarah describes her immediate arrival into all white, brightness, and comfort, my first impression is that she may be in the angelic realm. As the regression therapist, I must remain patient and allow what comes next to unfold. Then Sarah explains that her HS resides at the level of Source, which speaks volumes about her being an ARS. As always with my clients, I must combine the content that surfaces during the regression with what I learned about her personality and her current life during the interview.

Helper's huge smile is as wide as his whole face, filling my entire vision. He has white teeth and full red lips and is very happy. He's extremely tall with long arms and legs. What I see is primarily an enormous wide smile.

The souls where Helper and I come from have white wings! Helper is so tall that he's larger than earth. He is all white with such a happy smile. Helper's wings are enormous. My wings are smaller than his. I feel small, white, and feathered wings on my shoulder blades. My wings seem magical.

I have only had a few lives on earth, so I'm a beginner. I've had some lives not on earth to learn about and support IPS.

Helper emphatically tells me that his core energy is tied to pure love and compassion. When Dr. Backman asks whether my soul's energy is also characteristically pure love and compassion, Helper replies with a resounding yes.

• • • • • • •

Helper exudes great warmth with his smile. The combination of the vital amiable energy of the guide and the description of the guide and client with wings, and it's clear these are indicators that Sarah is an ARS. This client is unique as an ARS, given her small number of IPS, indicating her mission is to comprehend the vast wisdom of the celestial realm. Ancient knowledge and wisdom originate from the expansive universe before civilization on earth. Archangels arise from interplanetary existence with the corresponding identity in the ancient Egyptian teachings. Archangel Michael is the soul of the Egyptian leader and god Osiris.

I asked Helper where my husband, Michael, was right now. Helper says we can't see him, yet he is here. His energy is near; he is close to my energy right now. Helper tells me he is one of Michael's guides, as well as my guide. Helper is here to help both of us learn. I am told that Michael and I needed to learn to be incarnate as a deeply loving partnership.

Michael and I come from the same place in the celestial realm. Both of us are ARS. Michael is the Archangel Michael soul. Michael left his earth body because his soul energy was needed in the angelic realm. The portion of Michael's soul embodied on earth was needed to expand his HS. The Michael soul has the talent to work as a guide to people on earth.

At the soul level, Michael has wings. I also have wings at the soul level, but my wings are smaller than Michael's. Helper tells me that my purpose is to tell others about the story of the love between Michael and me. Michael is now my primary guide. Helper was my primary guide, but that changed when Michael completed his recent earth incarnation.

•••••••

Sarah's husband is close by. Romantic commitment embodied on earth between an archangel and an ARS is rare. The occasion when two humans join in a love relationship with a shared guide suggests a long-standing connection. When someone passes earlier than the statistical life expectancy, one potential explanation is that the percentage of soul energy the human brought into the body must return to support the HS.

Sarah's wings are smaller than Michael's because she is somewhat less evolved than Archangel Michael. People who knew Michael and Sarah in their human relationship expressed pleasure in feeling their bond. Our primary guide can shift within a lifetime, such as when Michael became Sarah's guide.

As I talk and write about my story of love with Michael, my pain of grief will lessen. My story of love with Michael is of a high quality. I will write the story of love and listen to the story. Listen to the songs he has been send-

ing, keep writing, and be with the light. The story comes from the light. Listen, and it will come. I am glad to know Michael is with me always. I am to keep tethered to Source while I am on earth.

I am talking now with Michael. I want to stay where I am. Please don't make me leave. Michael and Helper tell me I am permanently attached to the higher realm. I must believe this.

• • • • • • •

Michael and Sarah's honest and principled relationship in body is noteworthy. Michael is always intuitively and energetically accessible to Sarah. She is to assist others in believing in the shared attachment of two people in an egalitarian relationship of integrity and commitment. Source holds and projects the purity of respect and love as an essential component of a romantic relationship and how we treat all others. Sarah's pain at the loss of human Michael is equal to her ability to teach what romance with integrity truly is.

With my support, Sarah is guided to return to her body more fully. Embrace the following discussion I had with Sarah as I explain that having two angelic souls in a committed romantic relationship is rare.

Sarah: I've felt this high energy every time we have had a session. This time, it felt like one unit, from my hips to my feet. White light encased me.

Linda: That is the higher energy of Manu's mother energy. Creation. The unique nature of your marriage with Michael, an angelic soul, is unusual and was agreed upon by both your souls. I've not come across this situation before. The angelic realm has levels of evolution. Michael is an aspect of the soul of an archangel. Archangel Michael is the lead or head archangel.

Sarah: Yes, it is overwhelming to feel all the physical energy; all of it is enormous information to learn. You have helped me discover who I am and my purpose for staying. Thank you, thank you.

• • • • • • •

Sarah's soul regression is revelatory. However, it is challenging for Sarah to readapt her life without the human Michael. Never do I minimize the pain of having a dear person in our life transition, no longer available to have human conversation or touch. Michael and Sarah agreed to come together in life. Subsequently, they have also consented at the HS level to expand the perspective of others to comprehend what true and abiding love looks like.

Early wisdom and teachings on earth provide insight into advanced souls who guide humans and may incarnate. It is thought that Archangel Michael is the soul of Osiris of the Egyptian pantheon. Many believe that Osiris was an early ruler of Egypt approximately five to six thousand years ago. Osiris is the god of fertility, agriculture, and the afterlife; his image is depicted in many sacred Egyptian locations. A reasonable and likely assumption is that the soul of Archangel Michael was originally interplanetary, and he became the lead archangel directly serving Source.

In Summary

Grief and loss tied to the passing of a loved one or any other ending in our life can ferment our human self and soul self to grow or to fall into anger and despair. Choice in how we face loss leads to expansion or contraction. Losing a loved one can blind us to what might arise in the future, such as Madeline's experience rekindling a prior love. Our soul design related to past lives and our soul origin directly relates to how we traverse the grief journey. Anger, fear, and substances can block our expansion along the loss path. Surprisingly, grief and loss can make the sun shine brighter as we continue an incarnation.

Things to Think About

- Examine how the passing of a dear one altered your perspective and attitude toward life.
- Look back on signs you ignored that were indications of your loved one's communications.

- Consider who you have known in life today whose transition led to emotions that surprised you because you may have known that soul in prior lives.

Homework to Support Your Journey Through Loss

1. Have you been grieving, and has someone asked you why you are still holding on to your pain given that it's been over a year since the loss? Remember that there is no timetable for grief.
2. Do you sense that your loved one has communicated from the other side, and do others minimize your trust that the soul is immortal? Take this as an opportunity to stand in your integrity and offer education about the soul to someone else.
3. What elements of your soul design, such as past lives and soul origin, impact how you grieve?

CHAPTER NINE

Revealing Past-Life Karmic-Dharmic Themes to Evolve Humanity

> A woman in harmony with her spirit is like a river flowing. She goes where she will without pretense and arrives at her destination prepared to be herself.
>
> —MAYA ANGELOU

Our past lives and life purpose demonstrate the call for humanity's maturation as we evolve as individual souls and a community. Earthly life needs expansion, as well as a lack of judgmental attitude. Men are often nurturing and artistic, while women demonstrate business skills and independence. Expectations of how people should behave based on gender, skin color, financial status, and more must be altered and acceptance established. Your soul design, including past lives and soul origin, leads to your current-life agreements to balance past karmic freewill choices and utilize dharmic accomplishments. You have agreed to transform certain nonprogressive aspects of humanity.

Your Soul's Eternal Path from Immaturity to Higher Clarity

Western religious tradition suggests that the divine (the highest level of intelligent wisdom) and the soul are perfect. In contrast, spiritual belief in the East describes the goal of day-to-day life as transcending ego, human fear, and frailty to realize the true self, our oneness with the universal power. Perfection is an illusion of our minds and desires that implies something ideal and faultless. Neither the universe nor the most advanced soul is without blemish.

What is the purpose of being flawed? The answer is simple. Consider the following statement as your thoughts: "When it is clear to me that in this life or a past one, I've fallen down on the job by commission or omission, then—and only then—do I realize I must step up to elevate my behavior."

As we uncover past lives and reflect on our lives today, the reality of how we wish we had acted surfaces. My past lives include a role serving an autocratic government where I harmed and ostracized a group because of their religion. In addition, I have more than one life of placing my personal needs and wants above those of my spouse, children, and family. All of us have made inappropriate choices in past lives. The social structure of times in history may contribute to our actions. Nevertheless, as our soul evolves, we are expected, at times, to go against cultural norms and make more beneficial decisions.

Themes of humanity's ongoing need to mature and our soul history are ever present in my clients' regression descriptions. In this chapter, we will visit some of their past lives to personify areas of substantial evolutionary necessity. Reflect on your own life and contributions to equality, mind-body-spirit health, and solutions to conflict. Human action is the exclusive mode of how we, as a culture, can progress.

Soul evolution is a function of operating in the human body and making progressive choices. Just like we learn to add, subtract, and multiply by going to school to learn math, we expand our healthy attitudes and behavior through human embodiment. Discovering your past lives and soul origin leads to learning central themes essential to the evolution of humanity. What key threads of evolution have yet to be fully embraced on earth? How can we contribute to a healthy way of life on earth by balancing our karma and expanding our dharma?

As the Venerable Geshe Kelsang Gyatso states, *"Every action we perform leaves an imprint, or potentiality, on our very subtle mind, and each imprint even-*

tually gives rise to its own effect. Our mind is like a field, and performing actions is like sowing seeds in that field. Virtuous actions sow seeds of future happiness and non-virtuous actions sow seeds of future suffering. These seeds remain dormant in our mind until the conditions for them to ripen occur, and then they produce their effect. In some cases, this can happen many lifetimes after the original action was performed."

Karmic actions are the freewill choices we've made in past lives that were inappropriate to our soul's evolution and the evolution of humanity's development. We expand our dharma or soul accomplishment as we behave in wholesome ways. In each lifetime, our beneficial conscious actions become an indelible imprint on our soul, known as dharma. Such learning cannot be destroyed. Our soul climbs higher on the evolutionary ladder as we choose the right action on our planet. Soul regression opens a window to discern actionable themes essential to a favorable life. Your present-life and past-life challenges serve as occasions when you can choose to evolve and teach others about key needs in everyday circumstances.

Life purpose is determined with each ensuing incarnation. As we create a prebirth life contract, our life purpose or intentions for the upcoming lifetime include past-life karma and dharma. Often, during an embodiment, we satisfy our original life agreement with the option of an addendum or additional life commitments. SEP integrates our knowledge of soul design (past lives, origin, and archetype) with our present-life purpose. Our overall intention is to expand our soul evolution and the evolution of humanity.

MIRYAM: Past-Life Progress and Retooling

Miryam's soul regression and direction from her spirit guide reveal the progress and benefits of her conduct in a particular past life. At the same time, Joseph, Miryam's guide, suggests she could have made different relationship choices in the past incarnation that are specifically tied to her life today. As you follow Miryam's regression, consider the concept of women promoting equality with their primary partner.

I'm a woman riding a horse with someone riding right alongside me. This man is my husband, wearing jeans, a red-checkered shirt, and boots. He has long black hair. I feel exhilarated to be enjoying time with my husband. We've not been married for long. He has a nice smile.

Now it is years later. I am with my husband and two children, ages three and five. Life is a bit boring; I don't work. But my marriage is good. I want to go back to work, but I don't know what to do because my husband worries about the kids if I do return. Still, he is supportive.

I become a teacher, and I love the kids I teach. Then a few years go by. My children are off to college now. I am ready for change, but my husband does not understand. I want to move, but he does not want this. At the beginning of our marriage, I felt free, like on the day we rode horses together.

• • • • • • •

As you read Miryam's comments about her initial happiness and long-lasting relationship, keep in mind that her guide is aware of her positive attitude. Spiritual guides want to support both members of a relationship.

I've thought about leaving my marriage, but I am afraid. What will happen if I leave? Can I survive? My husband and I start to fight, and I know that I have to leave. I go back to the ranch where we rented the horses and get a job there. When my children are older, they come to live at the ranch. I have many different responsibilities at the ranch. Over time, the woman who owns the ranch decides to sell it to me.

Now it's the last day of my life. I'm in bed and looking out the window. My son and daughter are with me. I'm angry and not ready to go. I still need more freedom. My former husband says he's sorry we couldn't work things out. We have many regrets, but he struggled to give me much freedom. Still, I missed him and the years we could have had together after I left him.

I'm leaving my body behind now. I have died. I'm going up, and it is very light. There's someone with me now. He has a white robe and hair. He has open arms. This is Joseph, my teacher in the spiritual realm. He's ready to talk to me about the past life I just completed.

Joseph tells me that I did well with the responsibility of owning the ranch. Then Joseph scolds me, but everything he says is couched in love. He tells me that, at times, I focus too much on myself rather than on the needs of others. I gave in too quickly to have freedom and left my marriage. It was vital that I continue expressing my need for independence to my husband. Joseph tells me I needed to be closer to my children to guide them.

Joseph says I must work on my responsibility to others and make personal sacrifices. Still, he supports me and sends me love.

•••••••

Miryam is shown a past life where she was too hasty with her personal decisions. She allowed her need for freedom and her fear of being held down by her marriage to cause her to run away. Miryam avoided facing the challenge of seeking positive change in her marital relationship. In addition, the needs of her children were not a priority. Miryam's guide is wise in discerning how to express guidance. In some relationship situations, the woman must step away.

When we live in a human body, it is all too easy to be overcome by our human wants and desires rather than behave in a way that serves the deeper context of our soul learning. Our spirit guides press us not to take the easy road. When we are willing to choose the more challenging path of confidently expressing our need for equal power in a relationship, we contribute to both our soul evolution and humanity.

In a subsequent past-life regression, Miryam is a woman again, this time in a region rife with political unrest. She is hiding for safety in a cave with others when a soldier comes to save and protect her. Eventually she marries the soldier, and they have a child. Miryam discovers that the soldier is the same soul as a man with whom she is romantically involved in her present life. Today, this man's cultural beliefs cause his mother to stand in the way of the relationship because Miryam is not of the same background. Miryam is confronted again with examining her needs and standing in her power.

When Joseph steps forward at the completion of the regression, he explains that Miryam wishes to have complete freedom or be saved and protected by the man in her life. Miryam is to learn to be solid and stable, whether in a romantic relationship or not. She must learn to find a balance of equals, where she and her partner have stability separately and together. Neither complete freedom nor protection, moment by moment, creates a healthy daily partnership. An essential lesson in valuing our own needs, as well as the needs of others, is brought to light as our soul evolves.

Ask Yourself

What continued expansion of divine feminine energy, attitude, and laws are necessary on earth now? How do you contribute to meeting those needs? If you are a man, how do you support the divine feminine? If you are a woman, how do you support the divine masculine?

Divine Feminine and Divine Masculine: Humanity's Growth Process

Ancient cultural belief includes a divine feminine concept. Egyptians have Isis; the Greeks have Aphrodite; the Hindus have Shakti; Judaic Kabbalah has Shechinah; and Christians pray to Mother Mary. Still, the United States has never had a female president; most ascended master guides are referred to with male energy; the pope and cardinals are all men; God is viewed as male; and fewer than a third of all the United Nations countries have ever been led by a woman.

Qualities of the divine masculine include leadership, resilience, logical thinking, protectiveness, purposefulness, accountability, and emotional strength. Divine feminine attributes are intuitive, heart centered, compassionate, creative, sensual, and kind, as well as being versus doing and placing the needs of others over yourself. Add the soul archetypal seven-quality sequence of leadership, compassion, scholarship, aesthetic creativity, organization, group cohesion, and sustainable humanitarianism into the mix. Ask yourself if you share the entanglement of archetypal energies that seem stereotypically masculine or feminine. Of most significant importance is aiding others in shedding old-school, nonproductive biases. The point is that women and men both exhibit leadership qualities. Consider releasing any stereotypes you hold that men are to be strong leaders and women are to be strong nurturers.

What is healthy behavior? What is our soul nature? What has led our human culture to deny women the right to vote, secure a job with equal pay, or accomplish other goals by denying the equality of men and women? To comprehend, we must delve into the history of patriarchy on earth. All embodied souls are responsible for advancing human culture beyond the denigration of any group.

Kaylee, my next client, carries the soul archetype of compassion. Her guide mandates her to uphold the energy of love and acceptance of all people. In Kaylee's present life, she is in a leadership role where she can utilize her soul nature for the benefit of others. Through her female body, my client demonstrates classic male and female behavior that serves the needs of her life contract. In the regression narrative that follows Kaylee's, solving conflict requires stereotypical male and female aspects. Some say "necessity is the mother of invention" is a silly proverb. The necessity in our human culture is to honor both masculine and feminine traditional behaviors in balance to bring forth equality and lack of harm.

KAYLEE: Bringing Forth the Great Mother

I'm in an office; somebody is sitting behind a desk. I'm supposed to sit across from them. They look like a wooden toy that seems masculine. It's almost like a kid's toy you put together with blocks. He says, "I'm in charge of your marching orders." He shows me some paperwork. There's a picture of a colorful xylophone, like a toy. He says, "I want you to learn to play this. It's easy. You'll have no trouble."

He shows me page one and step one to learn to play this instrument. This is about hearing tones. He tells me I'm going far away and need to recognize these tones. I am going to earth. He's reluctant to say where we're going, which is far away. He tells me we must take that up to a higher level. He says I am from a location near Ibiscus, which is icy and mountainous.

But he tells me that he's not sure where my HS resides. He tells me to call him Edward and that he handles the marching orders for souls from Ibiscus and other interplanetary settings.

Edward explains there is a lot of stimulation where I'm going. He wants me to be aware of sounds and smells. He shows me a page of instructions for each of the senses, such as sight, sound, and smell. It helps if the soul has some exposure. Edward describes my first life on earth in India. Going to earth can be a challenge, no matter where you go. Edward suggests I go to the Great Mother to discover more details of where my HS resides. He says I know the way.

•••••••

Edward is a caring and supportive intermediary for Kaylee's primary guide. The cartoonlike descriptions of him indicate that my client is likely an IPS. Edward's role is to prepare IPS for their upcoming embodiment. Kaylee must be equipped to cope with her sensory experiences on earth, which is rather unfamiliar and entirely different from her place of soul origin.

I'm with the Great Mother as she speaks to me: "I am always pleased to reconnect with you and exude my love and presence. Your HS resides where I am, deep in the cosmos, all golden light. My daughters, like yourself, and I hold the feminine energy of the universe. We're so deep in the cosmos, surrounded by darkness. Many discount our existence. There have been many battles belittling our role and significance.

"I am connected to earth through my incarnate daughters. You would describe where I am as interplanetary. You are on earth now for several reasons. I need to understand more of what is happening on earth to prepare more souls to carry healthy feminine energy. My incarnate daughters gather information for me. Also, you are on earth to shift energy because it is so needed. You are a bringer of vigorous divine feminine perspective and behavior."

•••••••

Divine feminine energy and its acceptance are lacking on earth. Both women and men risk minimizing their conventional feminine perspective. Great

Mother communicates her potent stance of integrity and need. On earth, women and their characteristic attitudes have often been maligned. Kaylee is to use her life and platform to help humanity shift.

> *We chose a very traditional parental setup for you. Your father is attached to the patriarchal ways. We wanted you to be supported with stability and to see the pain and limitations of gender roles. We picked your parents accordingly.*
>
> *You've only had five or six earth lives. I have seven daughters, called the Seven Sisters. I always have seven on earth that represent completeness and power. You do not know any of the seven currently. All seven are not yet ready to meet one another. There are also two young boys as an added dimension to my work. The boys will embody the divine feminine like the seven daughters. I want you to meet the boys. One of the boys could come to you and your partner as a child of yours.*
>
> *There is so much heartache and discontent in the cosmos. I came into being around the time that intelligent life began on earth. I am the purveyor of divine feminine energy. When there is dualism, meaning male and female, somebody needs to hold the space for the feminine. The physical differential of human males and females causes battles on earth and elsewhere. Your job is to anchor the divine feminine on earth. Please stay awake in your life and travel to create expansion of the necessary energy on earth.*

•••••••

Take a moment to consider your life. It's likely your parents operated in conventional roles tied to their biological gender. Kaylee learned about the patriarchy at the most impressionable time in our lives, before age five. Great Mother is crystal clear about the preplanned intent for Kaylee's soul expansion to have parents as homemakers and breadwinners, respectively.

Kaylee's inexperience with life on earth manifests in perplexity about how humans are critical of one another. The Great Mother explains she has seven souls in female bodies on earth as emissaries of divine feminine energy. Seven is a sacred number with days of the week, chakras, soul archetypes, rainbow colors, and more. Also, two young boys are on earth as males to convey compassion. With precision, Great Mother expresses her concern about the duality humans have created with the expected behaviors laid on women and men. Unhealthy male behavior is displayed as dominance and power over others. Souls in female bodies display unwholesome actions, including self-minimizing and manipulative behavior toward others. Men and women must live in their power and trust their value.

In contrast to Kaylee's regression, Bill's revelation demonstrates the beneficial and damaging elements of stereotypical female and behavioral conduct. Kaylee is to teach women that demonstrating healthy emotions of mercy and warmheartedness is a strength. Bill's soul regression teaches negotiation to balance the needs of both parties versus war, and brutality illuminates healthy behavior.

BILL: A Soldier's Lot

During Bill's initial interview, he explained that a military background is not part of his current life and clearly stated that war is not the way to peace. In the opening scene of his past life, he is wearing a dark blue uniform as a young man in his late twenties. During the Civil War, he is an officer in the Union Army involved in a meeting with his superiors at the end of a difficult battle.

Hundreds of Confederate soldiers are being slaughtered. Some Union soldiers are also dead. As the young officer, I'm rebuffed by the general and colonels after telling them the war needs to be over and that there is too much useless killing. I'm a lieutenant and must return to my responsibility to lead the troops under my command. My wish is to defect, but duty prevails.

Another battle is being strategized where a Confederate camp will be boxed in by Union soldiers and taken by surprise. This next battle is, again, a massacre. During the fighting, I encounter a Confederate lieutenant like me. We look into each other's eyes, and I send the unspoken message, "We've got to stop this war." I'm shot by the opposing lieutenant in the leg and stomach and severely wounded.

While in the hospital, a senior officer visits and praises me as a hero and bestows a medal. I don't want the medal, so I am considering returning it. I believe that stopping the useless killing is impossible, so I'm discharged at my request. I return home feeling despair and depression and find it impossible to release overpowering memories of the horrific war. One day, while working on the farm, I sit down at the base of a tree and will myself to die of a broken heart.

••••••••

In examining the past life, Bill points out that it felt wasted. He did not understand the politics of war, which was said to be about glory and ego but turned out to be sad and senseless. As a young person in his present lifetime, Bill was determined to have a military career but soon chose not to pursue this vocation. He found the notion of war excessively uncomfortable and knew he could not fight in a battle. When friends in his youth invited him to see war movies, Bill would repeatedly decline without being able to explain why.

Finally, during the regression, the pieces fell into place in his mind and heart, and he understood his reasons for avoiding military life and war. "War is useless and never leads to peace," he explained. Furthermore, he could identify the soul in his present life, the Confederate lieutenant. This recognition provided Bill with an additional release.

Glory and ego as aspects of power over, compared to power within. When people recognize that all of us are powerful and must live in equality, honoring our life intentions, humanity will evolve. Divine feminine and masculine describe belief in ourselves and our natural qualities.

Countless soul regression clients discuss forced marriage. Details of each client's past-life situation describe the father intending to coerce his daughter to marry a middle-aged man who owns land nearby to intertwine assets and power. Once again, we come upon a destructive issue of ego and control. My client is almost always a woman in life today.

Human freewill choice is in play again as the higher realm does not condone required marriage. An additional component in most clients' past lives is the young woman falling in love with someone not in the same station. The genuine love relationship has been clandestine and often continues under the radar even once the forced marriage occurs. Ponder the purposeful objective of the higher realm in revealing past-life romantic relationships, seeking to guide each client's path to bringing divine and well-balanced feminine strength to earth.

MARIAH: Forced Marriage for an Angelic Realm Soul

I'm alone in a room. I'm wearing navy slippers and striped pajamas. I'm a girl about twelve years old with shoulder-length blonde hair. I'm afraid. There is smoke in the room. I was asleep and just woke up. I can't see, so I drop to the floor to crawl. I'm coughing. I make my way down a hallway. It's getting hotter, and I can't think clearly. I manage to go downstairs and get outside.

My house is burning, and then it collapses. I'm crying, and I feel in a mental fog. Now, there's a black man who is checking on me. I'm white, but not a child of the wealthy family who owns this plantation. I get along with the slaves. The slaves are trying to put out the fire. The white people are okay with the loss.

I live near here. Someone took me in like a foster family. He's a man who is like a mentor who taught me about math and science. Girls don't usually learn this type of thing. I'm sad I was asleep and didn't wake up soon enough to help him. The fire feels like arson to kill the man who was helping me. I feel intuitive, and I wish I had known what would happen.

It's later, and I'm twenty-four now. I'm wearing a dress and on horseback. After the fire, I was taken in by the aristocratic plantation owner's family. I've come to meet a man and get off my horse. I kiss the man. I'm a well-dressed woman, and this is where we meet in private. I'm different when I'm with him. Society has groomed me to be of a higher standing, so we can't be together. This is our secret meeting place.

I tell him I am being forced to marry someone I don't love. My family is at a high level in the community, and I don't know what to do. We both know I must do what I'm told. If I get married, instead of staying with this man I am with now, it is how I will stay alive. He understands and gives me a necklace, and I put my grandmother's ring on it. In that way, no one will question it. Nobody knows the necklace came from him. I will wear the necklace for the rest of my life, but I'm sad about leaving him.

•••••••

Mariah's past life has two key revelatory elements that guide her ongoing soul evolution in life today. She has a life during the era of slaves in the American South when white, moneyed people had power over blacks and lower-income whites. Mariah assimilates the value of love, knows no racial boundaries, and is boosted by a unique math and science education. Plus, she is confronted with the oppression of women who are forced to marry for the family's position rather than love.

It's later. I'm fighting with the man I married, and he slaps me across the face. I told him about the necklace, and that's why he's so angry. He's drunk and tells me he's wasted his life on me. This is normal behavior for him. I'm tired of this and want to kill him. Women work for us in our house just outside my bedroom door. They're worried about me.

The next night, I woke up for him. He comes into our bedroom very drunk. I act tired. He picks up the fire poker and hits me. I've had enough of him telling me I'm no good. He doesn't stop hitting me and says I'm to blame for his unhappy life. I've told the women who care for me about his behavior. He keeps hitting me with the fire poker until I'm no longer moving. He kicks me and plunges the poker into my abdomen. He gets the women who work in the house to clean the mess up so nobody knows about it. I have died. The past-life husband is the soul of a man I was with in my current life, and I ended the relationship.

The women take off my necklace. They find the man I love. He's heartbroken but is happy I'm not suffering the abuse. Now, I can leave this life.

•••••••

Past-life explorations can positively affect our attitude and actions in life. Unfortunately, physical, emotional, and sexual abuse are long-standing poor freewill choices in human culture. Source, the evolved guidance of earth, incessantly seeks to influence human behavior to adopt actions of the highest value for all. Prepare now to find powerful and pertinent details of Mariah as a soul.

> *I feel myself going up through layers of pastel colors and clouds. I'm being cleansed. I come to a temple, walk through the doors, and sit cross-legged. I am asked how I felt about my past life. I tell them that I lost myself the night of the fire when the man who supported me died. My twelve-year-old self sits down in front of me.*
>
> *The man who taught me science and math shared what he was learning. I'm to disseminate this information. The man channeled universal wisdom about how our world works using science and math. These details are to be brought to others. Now I see the image of a church that was in opposition to the scientific information. I'm to reveal valid, logical concepts about life and the universe. This life happened in the United States in the 1800s. In my life today, I now understand why various scientific guides have popped into my awareness.*
>
> *Now I'm being told to reintegrate my twelve-year-old self. She was innocent and full of wonder. As my younger self returns, I feel my angelic presence returns. I am to return to all I am. I am to stand in my authentic truth and be myself.*

•••••••

Mariah continues to impart essential components of necessary human evolution. Education for women and men is equally critical, as both must own their capability and power. Your skin color has nothing to do with your value as a soul, both with your HS and in the body. Trauma, at any point in our life but particularly in childhood, can leave us devastated and lacking capable physical and emotional energy. As the soul of valued scientists intuitively communicates with Mariah, she receives direction to utilize her sacred geometric knowledge.

> *Archangel Gabriel comes toward me and tells me I must be in the fullness of all I am. I see myself with bright gold shiny wings. Gabriel merges with me so I regain the memory of all that I am as a soul. I'm being told it will help me focus on being in my human body and bonding more closely with*

my HS. Archangel Gabriel reveals that I am an aspect of Gabriel incarnate on earth. Gabriel explains there are critical times when he chooses to embody on earth. It is a crucial time right now.

Gabriel tells me that some human relationships have made it more challenging to be in my compassionate angelic energy because some people have misunderstood my energy. Gabriel believes I am ready to live in my core energy of deep nurturance of all living things on earth. I am to help others to hold the highest light on earth.

•••••••

Between-lives soul regression brings the client front and center with the core of soul and human self, or as Mariah's guides say, the fullness of who we are. My client discovers that she is an ARS and is an aspect of the archangel Gabriel's soul. Thus she contains the energy of one of the leaders of the angelic realm, whose undertaking is to encourage and guide humans to usher in the highest action of divine feminine and divine masculine strength. As each of us lives our true essence, some may misinterpret our zeal.

Ask Yourself

When you or your child were in a committed romantic relationship, did you have an independent choice of a partner?

Humanity's Evolutionary Themes Continued

I appreciate Cathy's regression as she gains insights and finds out she is on earth now with sizable intent. In my work, people often ask me why there is suffering on earth. Not to minimize life's challenges, but the degree of suffering we experience directly equates to whether we view life as a glass half empty or half full. Suffering is the sandpaper of human existence. I always suggest we must honor our emotional and physical pain while not becoming wholly mired in it—no doubt there is human trauma on earth. Absorb Cathy's description of soul themes in our earthly life such as expanding love, being a healer on earth, allowing the flow of financial abundance, and blocking energy with light.

CATHY: A Mission and a Vow

Catherine, at age eighty-eight in her past life, quickly leaves her body and journeys across the veil into the spiritual realm. She finds herself as a soul above her past-life body, communicating via energy with her past-life daughter, who has been by her side during the dying process.

I am somersaulting in space. It is light, and I can see all the planets. I fall into a cloud of light, and it envelops me. Other spirits and I are chasing each other. It is fun. I love to float around. I play with a cat.

Now they want me to stop playing. Tall skinny people arrive. They look like four kings. They are like the hand of God. They tell me that I do meaningful work. They say that not all souls wish to come to earth. It is a labor of love to come here. It is a sacrifice to come to earth, for there is trauma here. Trauma spurs change. You can choose trauma during an embodiment. You can sacrifice yourself so that others are inspired to change. There is often pain involved with coming to earth.

They say they will now show me the soul group to which I belong. Fifty are the helpers, such as angels, teachers, and guidance counselors. The four souls who look like kings are the coordinators of my large soul group. They are my council of wise elders.

To gradually shift the third dimension (life on earth), we must have souls incarnate on earth. We must have people there to do that. Souls will wish to return to earth if the experience is of love. "You, Catherine, can make a change on earth. You must remain focused with your hand on the rudder. We will give you ample support." I like to play in the clouds. They nearly made me return to earth, but I am willing to go.

"The money you will need today will flow with the right intention. Your intent is always to solve actual environmental troubles on the earth." (This comment by Catherine's team is directly tied to her current work involving soil and water.) "You have done this work before. You serve as a doctor to the universe. You are to help the universe remain functional in literal and figurative terms. Continue with your work as it is now."

•••••••

Numerous clients describe the energy of Source (God, Great Spirit, the Manu) as four highly advanced IPS who strive to guide humans. Consenting to embody on earth suggests that Cathy is an ARS, even though only some of the members of the angelic realm ever arrive into earth embodiment. Thus, Cathy's soul pod is the angelic realm. Cathy's story illustrates how opportunity for abundance is possible when we live our soul agreements in alignment with our soul essence. Love is required for humanity's well-being. Science, which is tied to caring for soil and water, is essential as Cathy focuses on her literal work in life.

> *Dark energy is where there is no light energy. You are to help keep the universe and energy alive. God is a structure of energy. Love is pure energy. When the structure of energy does not flow, there are kinks. The kinks cause us to feel negative emotions. You can help repair the kinks. We need to bring positive intent back to earth. This will open the flow of positive emotion, the flow of love.*
>
> *We will be sending new people to assist with your work. As you work directly with the elements of the earth, more people will feel love. Healing, both literal and emotional, will occur. Souls with significant power will create a blanket of energy. We all need to feel love much of the time.*
>
> *The pleasures of incarnation are to be felt. You must both work and play. It makes us ill by restricting our play. Look at work as play. There are no failures.*

•••••••

Catherine is an example of a person with a powerful and profound mission in this lifetime, revealed in her soul regression. Clear-cut revelations demonstrate her covenant to block dark energy by holding fast to the light of love, compassion, and truth. Where light energy exists, the dark cannot cross the threshold. An alternate way of presenting this message is that love, belief, and compassion supersede fear, despair, and anguish.

All souls have a vital purpose, no matter what the script is for their present incarnational experience and regardless of their degree of soul development. Catherine grasps who she is at the soul level and why she has taken up her current life's work. I have included content from her session in part to illustrate how to make a vow to serve humanity. Her regression skillfully indicates the need to heal natural resources in our planetary environment. Furthermore, her words, while closely linked with her soul via hypnotic regression, were like an oration, or speech, from the other side.

Catherine conveys profound and critical esoteric details about our planetary needs. From the standpoint of our earth and its atmosphere, we have only to examine the environmental news and the growing evidence today to become aware of the ecological damage occurring. The natural order is increasingly out of sync. Catherine is a healer, not unlike a massage therapist or an acupuncturist.

The universe can also ease energetically and metaphysically. Examples cross our human paths daily, showing there is not enough love on this planet: crime, drug abuse, social injustice, political turmoil, racial hatred, and genocide; the painful litany could go on. As a hydrologist, Catherine agreed to serve literally in healing planetary earth, air, and water. During her regression, she is instructed to work with the flow of love energy. Catherine is an ARS in the guise of an everyday person, offering love to the environment and to individuals.

Now comes an additional theme to explain why many, if not most, people seeking spiritual knowledge are inclined to hide their consciousness of deep intuitive intelligence. Gregory's regression elucidates a past life of hidden knowledge in a period when many feared those with healing and instinctual abilities.

Ask Yourself

Do you believe you are aligned and do not block your financial abundance? In the broadest sense, what actions do you take to be the healer of humanity?

Gregory receives validation to explain his life as a formally trained medical practitioner and a healer, having had profound, intuitive, telepathic experiences from early childhood. As you absorb Gregory's past-life account, consider your potential past-life experiences that give rise to your interests and emotions in life today.

GREGORY: A Wizard and Healer

I am speaking to the king. I am his advisor, and I tell him that if he goes into battle, it will be a disaster. The king is concerned, but he knows he must go into battle. I am telling him that if he does this, everything will be lost and dispersed as a result. He feels caught in the politics of the time.

So we are planning to be safe for his wife and children and for the wisdom of the ages. There is a piece of wisdom that is guarded. It cannot go into the hands of the invading French. I look like Merlin, a wizard, and have a mystery school. I am teaching others about healing, alchemy, and energy mastery. If the French get hold of this information, they may misuse it. A lot more destruction could happen. So this must be safeguarded.

The battle ensues, and everything moves quickly. There is a scene of rushing into the castle and taking scrolls of information, crystals, and the like. I take the scrolls and must hide them. I go deep into the woods to a place where no one can find me. This is an invisible zone I have created.

I am under pressure to keep this information safe. I am sad that the world has become embroiled in chaos and mayhem. I know that I am planting the seed for the future by taking this information and burying it. It looks like somewhere in the British Isles, like England, Ireland, or Wales. It is time to move forward. As I hide this knowledge for safekeeping, I know I will return to it sometime in the future.

•••••••

This past-life detail provides a clear example of the alchemy of spiritual truth. Throughout history, many cultures, such as Atlantis, Lemuria, Egypt, Mesopotamia, and India, have known the core consciousness of all that is. Because of the lack of support and fear of other humans, such deep wisdom has gone underground, only to surface many years later when perhaps the time and climate were more suitable.

In Summary

Your soul design, combined with your present-life blueprint, is a collage representing critical components of your soul, including themes of your past lives and your intended contribution to the essential advancement necessary for humanity at this time. Merging the artistry of your soul design with your current-life happenings and freewill choice brings forth your evolution and the evolution of our global community. Consider your life today promoting gender, lifestyle, ethnic equality, lack of fear, trust in the flow of abundance, and conscious, spontaneous, intuitive wisdom as a formula to progress humanity and all living things distinctly.

Things to Think About

- When you stand firm and believe you contribute to augmenting divine masculine and divine feminine human behavior, you bring balance to earth.
- Trust you know your soul origin as EBS, IPS, or ARS and why you are on earth now.
- Acknowledge your passionate actions today to realize your dharma of past lives.

Homework to Understand the Themes You Are Balancing on Earth

1. Use your journal to capture your actions in the last month meant to balance the divine feminine and masculine.
2. In what manner are you a healer in your current life?
3. What actions of freewill choice do you make that your parents did not?

CHAPTER TEN

Living Each Day: Your Soul Essence and Design

> I alone cannot change the world, but I can cast a stone across the water to create many ripples.
>
> —MOTHER TERESA

Your soul is intelligent living energy animating your body. A portion of your soul resides within your body and is energetically tethered to your HS in the elevated realm of your origin. All elements of your soul design, including past lives, soul ray, soul origin, and soul pod, are imprinted into your HS. Your spiritual guide functions with your HS to support your life agreements. When on earth, you always have free will to act based on your life contract.

No other soul is identical to you. Our soul design is intricate, complex, and unique, brought forth through skills, passions, fears, and desires. With knowledge of our tapestry, we can follow our hearts and abilities and alleviate concerns explained by past-life events to live our best and destined selves.

SEP illuminates the power and development of your soul, reflected in your everyday human self and the wisdom your HS has attained. In French, intuition is described by the word *clairvoyance*, which means you have the clear ability to vision outside your immediate surroundings. Intuitive information comes to us through all our senses, whether mental imagery, emotion, body sensation, smell, or simply a sense of knowing. Everyone is intuitive. Yet the more advanced your soul evolution, the more your intuition will be accessible. All you need to expand your intuition is practice and trust. Tuning in to learn the critical details of our past lives or the content of our prebirth contract, or to communicate with loved ones or guides in spirit, is done by using our divinely inspired intuitive receptors. Your intuitive capability will serve you well during regression or when utilizing a spiritual practice to uncover elements of past lives and receive direction from your HS and guide.

SEP directs you to explore your past lives, examine the components of your life agreement, receive direction from your spiritual guide and HS, know your soul origin, and grasp your themes of learning and evolution. To know yourself as a soul in past lives, your origin, guide, and more, you must choose to practice and expand your intuitive ability, along with soul regression. SEP is an insightful tool that can meld your past lifetimes and soul skills with who you are today, with intentional passion and spiritedness. You will evolve and enhance humanity's consciousness by bringing together all you are in past embodiment, immortal soul qualities, and current-life commitments.

SEP is a revolutionary and evolutionary approach to studying, revealing, and utilizing the knowledge held in your immortal soul. Conventional psychology focuses only on your current life. Imagine having only a one-inch square view of a glorious sunset or a famous painting like Monet's *The Artist's Garden*. Without SEP to reveal your soul design, you know 25 percent of who you are at best.

Stepping Into Your Power: Unveil Your Soul Design

Envision your soul's journey like a camera with three lenses. One lens is trained retrospectively, on your significant past lives. The viewfinder of the middle lens shows precisely what's happening in the moment of now. You have a third lens on the future, which must be flexible. Events in our life today weave together our past-life history, including karmic elements in need of balance, our prebirth soul agreement, and the freewill choices we make daily. This tapestry illuminates the lens that presents potential future-life details and subsequent incarnation options. Upcoming lives are possibilities directly affected by how you live today's life. My foremost message is that each of us has the power to influence what happens from this moment onward. When your soul design comes into focus, you can receive guidance and create an evolutionary life embracing who you are as a soul.

Here, a soul regression client explains.

> *My guide tells me my commitment to care for my ninety-two-year-old mother and walk alongside her until she completes this lifetime is for the soul evolution of us both. A past life is revealed where the soul of my mother today was my ten-year-old daughter whom I abandoned. I died of a broken heart when my husband, her father, left me. Now we are balancing the karmic remnants of the past incarnation by ending the conflict we've had in our present life. I voluntarily care for my mother in peace while she is open to receiving my nurturance.*

•••••••

In each life, we are brought face-to-face with mending opportunities tied to past lives. What comes of our future is inextricably tied to using awareness of our past to heal in the present and step boldly forward in our ongoing ascent to higher wisdom through soul evolution. Without knowledge of your soul design, you are handicapped and unaware.

Past Lives, Soul Archetype, and Your Purposed Prebirth Agreement

Each life is another play in which our soul is the actor. We choose behavior for our soul's evolution and to advance humanity. At the soul level, you consent to a prebirth agreement crafted by you and your guide. As a soul, we take on a physical vehicle called the body to begin a new incarnation. An overall life plan is created, including past-life karma you intend to balance and past-life dharma or accomplishments you seek to utilize to accomplish your purpose. Each key person in your upcoming embodiment is chosen by mutual agreement. Family, friends, and mentors are often souls with whom you've interacted in past lives.

You are the leading actor with a personality specific to each life. Your soul has an immortal signature nature. The character we embody in each life play is temporary, while the soul carries our everlasting note. To step moment by moment through the life we are to live, the soul must gain some degree of symbiosis (in some plays more, in others less) with the body, melding its proper enduring temperament with the style of the person indicated in the script. The person in each play, or lifetime, is thus an amalgamation of eternal soul nature and human personality traits attached to a dispensable body and brain.

Your soul signature is an archetype of seven possibilities you carry out in every incarnation, whether with a public platform or a neighborly intent. You might be keenly focused on change, whether for earth life or in a narrow fashion for your family. If so, you are a ray one soul. If you are a two, your ability to share love and compassion is palpable. As a three, your style is to learn incessantly, desiring to meld knowledge of your passionate interests. A four has an aesthetic and entertainment focus on music, cuisine, or artistry. When you know a five, you can count on them to organize and implement whatever is needed. Six energy is the strongest cheerleader for group cohesion, whether family, work, or the planet. Last, seven cares about all things humanitarian with perpetual evolution.

Our upcoming-life agreement often includes a specific blueprint to educate others, such as the need for international collaboration among countries or subsidized housing for seniors. In addition, even when someone's prebirth commitment includes the intent to work on the world stage, there are always more personal elements, like the commitment to healthy parenting. Life purpose for some is more general and possibly even less evident, but no less critical. As a result, some people may complete a soul regression session with crystal clear details in their conscious minds regarding their current-life purpose. Others come away from a session with a general sense of having decided to come into the body this time to serve as a healer in any manner they choose.

JEFF: Simple Nurturing

Jeff arrives for his regression, seeking answers to an obvious question: "What are my lessons to learn and unlearn in this life?" As the regression session progresses, he appeals to his council of wise elders to know more about his life purpose. Their response comes forward.

Your overall purpose in life is to nurture. You are to live simply. You are to have a relationship with and be connected to animals. You are to speak your truth. Be conscious. Just live in the moment. Do not judge. Be with people where they are at any point in their life. Take in warmth and sunshine. Let yourself grow.

•••••••

Jeff's marching orders suggest he is a soul archetype two. He is keenly aware of himself and the perspective on life he has developed as he nears fifty years of age. No frustration arises as he is handed details to follow in the continuing days of his productive working life and into the future with his retirement. Although Jeff is not directed toward any specific employment, he comprehends spirit's intention for him.

At first, the challenges of a past life may seem poorly planned and without objective. Spiritual guides provide an alternate perspective to what can look like complications or lack of success during a past life or in life today.

CAROLYN: Learning from Past-Life Happenings

There was a good reason why I lived a past life not being connected with my mother. I had to develop myself. I am gentle and courageous to have taken on such a tough life. Three guides come forward. The one in front is the spokesman. I call him Old Man. He wishes to talk; he is caring and connecting. He tells me it takes great courage to be what we are no matter what we do not receive. It takes great courage to know what we do not have. I have learned to be nonjudgmental about people and who they are or are not.

•••••••

Evolution out of deprivation may be the most grueling yet transformative mode of advancement. One of the most impactful books I have ever read is Viktor Frankl's *Man's Search for Meaning*, about his survival in a concentration camp during the Holocaust. Carolyn's regression is an eye-opening example of pulling oneself up by the bootstraps when there is no bond with the mother. Past-life experiences lacking what we ideally expect to have, such as love, nurturance, freedom, and health, are arduous yet expansive. Our spiritual support never leaves us.

Imagine a profound yet engaging conference among your HS and guides to develop an upcoming embodiment. As your soul evolution progresses, each upcoming life is driven more by your HS and less by your guides. When you are a young soul, your guides take primary responsibility for your incarnation details. Immersed in a body, you are implored to trust your intuition and the events and signs that point your life forward to new plans, people, and experiences. Your HS is always part of your guidance team and, at times, is the lead member of your support staff.

Ask Yourself

When and where did you live in a past life? What occurred in a significant past life that impacts you to this day?

Soul Origin: Your Higher Self's Base of Operations

An EBS has been evolving for hundreds of lives in an earth body, if not a thousand or more. Most EBS have had a small number of non-earth lives. As an EBS, I know several things about my past lives. All our lives are not significant. What is important are our lives of detrimental karma and accelerated dharma. EBS have lived during crucial points in earth's history, such as prehistoric times, early civilizations, the biblical Old Testament, crucifixion, and political revolutions.

Lives of challenge contain examples of our behavior as the victim and the victimizer. The abused, sadly, often becomes the abuser. Our current-life details reveal themselves through our memory, as well as through family members who can offer insight. Without the big picture of our string of past lives, it is impossible to fully comprehend why we must, for example, cope with a father who is an alcoholic or care for a child with a chronic illness. The soul of our father may have been the servant girl we abused, and our child may have been our child of the past whom we left to be raised by grandparents.

KYLIE: Self-Loss Due to Prostitution Without Personal Limits

Kylie, a woman in her fifties, discovers past-life trauma created through failure to protect herself from abuse. Kylie has not taken steps to accomplish vigorous separation from physical, emotional, and spiritual harm. Kylie has coped with unexplained back pain in life today because she hasn't developed the strength to stand up and say, "No, you cannot and will not take advantage of me."

I'm outside in the city; it's a chilly night. I have on a short tight skirt and a provocative top. My hat is classy; my hair looks nice. I solicit business and use the rooms upstairs. A man comes to get me; we negotiate payment. There are other prostitutes and men around. I'm cut off from my feelings, not present. For some reason, the women here ostracize me; I'm forced to leave. I have nothing.

It's later now, and I live in the country. I have a typical family. I don't deserve this because of the prostitution. I'm not in love with my husband; I married for survival. I have two children, a boy and a girl.

Now it's the last day of my life. My death is tragic; it's 1925. I'm the passenger in a car; there's an impact, and I die. My guide steps in—I'm told that even in life today I still don't understand that sex must be tied to a sacred contract between two people. When we sexually share ourselves, we've agreed at a soul level to come together, with our emotions and our spirit.

I'm still damaged by the experience of being a prostitute at age seventeen. In my current life, I also gave away my power at age seventeen when I became sexually active. The head of my council of chief elders arrives.

He tells me that the back pain I've struggled with for ten years is because I must strengthen my backbone, my ability to stand up for myself. I must speak my truth.

I am told that I don't set healthy boundaries for myself. In my life as a prostitute and other lives, including my current one, I have not been discerning. I think that I can gain love through sex. I must honor my need for healthy love. The man I am with today takes energy from me and does not give back. I let people take advantage of me. I don't honor my needs, so my back pain indicates that I don't seek the support I need from myself and others.

I'm also told that my diet must change. It would be best to eliminate sugar and wheat. I am to stabilize my blood sugar and exercise more; swimming is good for me.

Now the soul of my daughter, who was stillborn, comes to me; her name is Sharina. She says, "Come on, Mom." She takes me to a place of bright white light. It's as if I am taking off a bodysuit. Sharina is helping me leave the life of prostitution behind. Then she tells me thank you for carrying her to earth. It was a contract that I would carry her in my womb, and she would not survive at birth. Sharina calls herself an angelic ambassador; as an angel, she needed experience on earth that came from simply being here during my pregnancy.

•••••••

Kylie is given strict instructions to strengthen her fortitude and value herself, speak her needs, and release the trauma of sexual abuse. She must break the chain of past-life patterns to protect herself from continued abuse. The care and feeding of her body also must improve. In addition, Kylie is not at fault and is asked to let go of her grief over the passing of her baby. We learn that evolved souls sometimes come into body through the womb in pregnancy to gain a brief earth experience.

Interplanetary Souls: Extraterrestrial Roots

Martin's soul regression expresses the origin of an early intelligent lifeform on earth. Such precise details are calming to experience and provide a striking explanation of soul qualities.

MARTIN: An Intelligent Birdman on Earth to Expand Healthy Life

Upon meeting my client Martin, I noticed that his soul design qualities were immediately on display. He was born in southeast Europe and lived in numerous Middle Eastern, European, and North American countries. It is common that when someone has moved from place to place, they seek a comfort spot that is hard to find because they are not from earth. Furthermore, Martin has approximately ten animals and lives in a relatively small apartment with birds, cats, dogs, and a pig. To round out the picture, he is an attorney who works with legal issues related to earth's environmental malfeasance and standards. Martin's regression content sheds light on early advanced animal life on earth.

I'm outside in space, and the energy here is orange. I feel calm where there are golden lights. I'm sitting on some rocks. I don't have human feet. I look like a big bird called Birdman. I'm very old and dying. This is not earth.

Now, as the Birdman, I've died. I feel a lot of heavy armor, like a bodysuit, so it is hard to leave the body. This was the last form of that species, Birdman, off earth. He wanted to fly but did not know how to use his wings. A new form was created with a smaller body with lighter wings.

I look like a dinosaur with wings, and I can fly. Now I am on earth. I want to see how high I can fly. Around me are other forms of animals. I go home to the celestial realm, like a liquid-gold environment. At my home location, I am in a golden lake. I have changed to a liquid form. I am part of the lake, and the lake is my guide called Siriu.

Siriu tells me he created the first humanlike being to come to earth. The birdlike dinosaur that is my soul was the second humanlike being on earth. The first humanlike being was not attractive. We came to earth to feel sensation. We also came to learn about the land, air, and water to create the form best suited for planet earth. This happened thirty million years ago as we prepared for incarnation on earth.

I embodied a flying dinosaur; we were more intelligent and different than other dinosaurs.

All planets change over time. As earth evolved, we had to change our form. My soul had to be altered to a different form to return to earth. My soul group had to keep changing as earth modified over time. If my soul and those like me do not transform, we will not survive on earth.

Because earth was initially only rocky, Birdman had a hard shell and could manage. The Birdman's body had to suit the planet. My soul's form had no head at my interplanetary home location, so air and water were unnecessary. When water and air started to come on earth, Birdman was altered to have wings and a head to manage on earth.

My life purpose is to find other human and animal beings who come from my home location and bring them back together. While I am on earth with my group, we must do what we can to influence humans to better care for earth's environment. These souls are all from my original setting. I am not likely to return to earth incarnation. We must evolve, and we are losing our quality of life because of too much damage to the soul from earth's energy and way of life. My type of soul cannot survive easily on earth at this time because the conditions of life on earth are changing.

My guide tells me that Linda and I have met each other to help others find their soul family on earth. Some advanced souls that are IPS have not been on earth many times and need the support of their fellow souls. Many changes need to happen on earth, and very advanced souls in body must have all the bolstering they can find.

•••••••

It would be a golden opportunity for you to sit beside me during a regression while surprising soul disclosure details flow from my client. I am blessed to receive a profound course in the soul.

Martin's regression is astounding and valid. With each soul regression client, I learn more beyond what I expect to receive. All souls who arrived in the earliest time of intelligent earth incarnation were interplanetary. I have often heard clients explain that earth is an experiment to determine whether humans can take adequate steps to develop a vigorous, flourishing human and environmental culture. Only the joint effort of most humans can shepherd and elevate a homogenous balance with a heterogeneous population. Our original intent for earth's progress has not been realized.

Martin's professional pledge is to create a healthy domain to support all life. He is hard-pressed to live on earth daily, remaining steadfast in his life's purpose. I know why I encounter people like Martin; they significantly need self-understanding and moral support to be who they are today.

ELIANA: Bridging Wisdom from Outside of Earth

Eliana's past life indicates the risk we often take, both in past lives and today, when we commit ourselves firmly and passionately, embedded in what we know in our hearts is right, no matter the cost. As expressed in the words *rearview mirror*, sometimes you must put that life truly in the past. In her journey, Eliana will consider what comes next, knowing we are not to cry over spilled milk but move forward with a reinvigorated recipe of change and advancement.

I am outside in the mountains, and it's cold. I wear leather pants, like a Viking, and my chest is bare. I'm a man about age thirty curled up in a ball. I know I'm going to die. I feel disappointed and defeated. My time has been wasted. I'm disgusted and sad. Leaving my wife and children is so difficult.

I've been outcast or excommunicated. I've been put out to die in the cold, and all my weapons have been taken. I'm not injured.

Now, I'm younger and live in a large hut with many people. I think I'm the leader of this group. I'm challenging something. I'm not okay with what is happening to my people. Other leaders don't care about the community. So I'm being overthrown. It doesn't matter that I'm trying to help our people. I know there's risk in what I'm doing. I must do what I believe is right.

Someone grabs me in the middle of the night. They're going to dispose of me. I'm concerned about my family and that they will harm my children. I've been dumped in freezing water. I feel disappointed that I failed.

My life was a waste because I couldn't accomplish what I needed to do. I failed. I don't feel attached to my human life.

I've died now. I can see my body curled up. Now I sense my guide and am so happy to see him. This guide feels like an old friend. That life is in the rearview mirror; it's over.

My guide feels grandfatherly. His name is Paul. Well, I call him Paul, but his name is Ezekiel. Paul was his name when I was with him in a past life. Paul is not my primary guide, but he chooses to demonstrate his presence and never-ending encouragement. My main guide is now greeting me. His name is Jophiel. This guide is twice as tall as Paul and is taking me somewhere. We're in an angelic hall of light where other souls are scribes.

I feel a level of comfort about the past life. Jophiel tells me he knew there was a chance I wouldn't succeed with what I wished to do in the past life. In that life, there was an opportunity for forward movement for everyone, like a quickening. I came to instigate that choice point. Going into that past life, I knew it was possible the collective wasn't ready to shift, but I agreed to act in that life. I agreed to trust the divine unfoldment of what would or would not happen.

I have some attachment to the fact that it didn't work. I'm being comforted by that. I'm being shown that my guides knew it was a possibility I wouldn't accomplish what was planned. I feel my energy is being rewired, and release is happening.

Jophiel tells me that he and I both have wings. The setting where we are in the spiritual realm is the home of my HS. I am aligned with my highest path to anchor the elevated vibration of light energy from Source. I'm being shown a tube that energy moves through, and I must keep it clean and open. It is a conduit that must be open and flowing. The energy comes from the divine and is a pure light channel needed on earth. It's a beam for others to tap into and receive. It's a power Source of light. I allow the light to move through me to bring it to our planet.

This light is connected to other locations in the celestial realm as a bridge merging the high frequency of wisdom from beyond earth. Others are doing this work like a highway among celestial locations containing the advanced wisdom of high souls. Souls from locations other than earth are committed to advancing our human culture.

I am told that I am serving humanity with the option to step into a more visible work capacity. This is not required, but I can choose to hold space and light. I would be supported from the highest level if I met my soul's objective.

Jophiel is a direct emanation and connection to Source. Jophiel always supports me. Jophiel is one level below what we often call God as an emissary of the highest guidance on earth. It took a lot of preparation for my soul to come to earth and remain attached to the light.

I'm being flooded with an immense amount of divine love and appreciation. I feel reverence and am being comforted. I'm tired a bit and am powerfully supported. Jophiel is with me to help transport the signal from Source. The work I am doing is happening in many star systems simultaneously. At this time, an aspect of my soul is present in multiple celestial systems doing similar work.

Jophiel explains that earth is guided by a specific energy called Source, God, Great Spirit, and other labels. Other celestial locations are led by their high frequency of direction. In other words, there are different and separate high guidance for other settings. Thus, there are multiple Sources in communication with one another.

I am told that I must live my life as I choose. My most significant purpose is to be a conduit of light for the earth. This is my life's mission. I have had much preparation in my past life to be here now. There must be a conscious choice for me to align with this high energy. I can materialize this advanced wisdom in whatever form and activity I wish to express. As I choose how to live my life, I can keep bringing in more light on behalf of Source.

There are others incarnate on earth who have a similar related objective. I can work in conjunction with others to unify and bring greater flow.

The energetic work I am doing is taxing. When I seek the company of others with similar missions, it will lessen the drain on my energy.

Finally, I am guided to align every morning with Jophiel and my attachment to the light. I am to state my intent for the day. I will feel the support of my guide and the highest frequency. I am always to trust.

•••••••

Eliana's guide, Paul, reminds us that we can have a secondary and a primary guide. Jophiel, an archangel and Eliana's primary guide, arrives to support her. The possible preincarnation understanding is that our intent to alter human attitudes may or may not come to fruition.

Eliana serves humanity's needs just by being incarnated on earth as a trench to allow high, evolved energy to flow to earth. Here's the crucial key: we can choose to tap into the high Source of elevated energy and wisdom to support all living beings, or we can ignore the available enervation of equality and caretaking.

An expanded possibility is for Eliana to share and teach the wisdom she receives from her ARS's home. As my client wholeheartedly encompasses the truth of her soul's origin, she must trust intuition to present options for her life today. Collaborating with others whose life intent is related will augment her work on earth. Jophiel is ready, willing, and able to provide stability and direction when needed. ARS on earth know they are different than many others but don't take on an attitude of judgment. During Eliana's preregression interview, she expressed her inner conflict from childhood forward of knowing she was different without context or guidance. Now, with an adequate paradigm of who she is as a soul, her daily life and actions take on meaning previously not understood. Elevation of all people remains painfully lacking in our earthly existence. Eliana now selects how to behave going forward with her life and intentions.

Ask Yourself

What do you love about yourself as an EBS, IPS, or ARS?

Soul Evolution: Grief, Relationships, Health, and Social Equality

Prepare to examine your present-day life for clues, if not billboards, that spotlight the themes of your current life that are related to your past lives, soul origin, and humanity's evolution. Grief and loss occur in everyone's life. Yet when an essential aspect of your life has dissolved, either through death or another means of ending that is outside the norm, realize that you are either cleaning up a past life issue or dedicated to teaching others how to face permanent change.

Examples of out-of-the-ordinary grief and loss include the passing or lack of one parent before your adulthood, the loss of your health from illness or injury in childhood, the demise of your child, homelessness, job loss, and other extraordinary endings. Past-life trauma asking for balance will rear its head in your life today through fears, unexplained illness, and repetitive and unexpected circumstances. If you attempt to ignore signs of loss without realizing you have emotional-spiritual work to do today, another indication of what you are to face will show up again.

I must admit from my own life, personal friends, and professional relationships that the hills and valleys of grief and loss are exquisitely complex and reshaping in ways we never anticipated. Our strength comes from somewhere beyond our wildest imagination to lead our transmutation. Alteration of who we thought we were and where we thought our life was headed only occurs when we dig deeply into the pain. I advise you to step away from those people who don't want to accept the gut-wrenching process you are facing and unequivocally embrace those who walk the journey alongside you.

Love Relationships of All Types

I hear a song: "Where do I begin to tell the story of how great a love can be?" Now think about people you love and have loved. Don't only consider romantic love. Expand the notion of loving someone to anyone, including your beloved pets. If you are an EBS, all your salient relationships are with souls you've known in past lives. For IPS and ARS, your pivotal relationships are likely with souls with whom you've shared lives, depending on how many earth and non-earth lives you've experienced.

When my psychologist colleague passed in 1993, I knew nothing about past lives, much less that I had shared several incarnations with his soul. Upon laying eyes on our first grandchild, a deep-rooted feeling surfaced and continues even more strongly now in his early adulthood. I urge you to step away from relationships that feel excessively toxic or limit the amount of contact with such persons. The reverse is crucial also: Take time to be in touch with those people of great value in your life, and don't let months or years go by without reaching out to them. I have a very dear girlfriend I've known since I was thirteen. Our worldviews, in specific ways, are substantially different. I love her just the same and want to be sure we communicate regularly.

Health: The Meaning of Crisis

Health and health fears once again are a window into past lives, today's soul evolution, being a teacher, soul origin, and more. Past lives explain health crises and fears. Did you die from choking three hundred years ago at age thirty-five? And so you have always feared having a severe choking episode? Did someone close to you in life today die by being shot or stabbed in the abdomen when you knew them in past life? You may have abdominal symptoms tied to your worry about repeating traumas and relationships from past lives in today's life.

Are you to teach others how to cope with a life-threatening diagnosis? Are you healing a past life when you harmed someone, and in life today, you have symptoms in your body tied to where they were hurt? If you are an IPS, do you have various health issues? You've not experienced many lives in the human body. IPS very often put up with physical complications, from simple to complex. Last, are you avoiding taking more time for rest and joy, resulting in a health concern that forces you to set aside time for yourself?

Our HS and guides are our wisest teachers. They will escort us to walk up to the mirror and see what we're consciously missing. Honoring our bodies is essential. Honoring our required individual soul evolution and the progress of humanity is also crucial. Find time to play regularly and seek joy. You are caring for your needs and demonstrating to others what is vital to maintaining a healthy life.

Social Equality

Earth life is out of balance in many respects. Make a list of times when you ignored the needs of an ethnic minority or a community with lesser means different than your own. When have you minimized your needs of recognition as a woman, or of women if you are a man? Relatedly, if you are male, do you allow your emotions to be known by those close to you? In what manner do you not take time to further the balance of all cultures and people from all walks of life? Humanity's expansion is crucial. Each of us has the power to create alteration of the holes in humanity's evolution.

Ask Yourself

Do you have a health issue that is tied to past lives? What do you do daily to manage your emotional and spiritual health?

Soul Essence Psychology: Soul Design Revelations and Strengths

As we have explored in this book, SEP requires the discovery of who you are beyond present-day life. The underpinning of SEP is your soul design, which captures your past lives, unique soul qualities and strengths, where you come from as a soul, and your reasons for being incarnated on earth to evolve humanity. Past life and between-lives soul regression with a trained, experienced therapist will aid the illumination of who you are as a soul, with strengths and past-life experiences to discover and release.

What are the benefits of exploration of your soul design? Depression, anxiety, and fears arise from current life and past life. Life today is inextricably intertwined with past lives, including people, experiences, and beliefs. To expand the picture, if you lived during the era of the crucifixion, you may be fearful of suffering harm for your faith or may be zealously tied to your beliefs. Fear today that seems illogical, lacking current-life rationale, is attached to events in past lives. For example, if you uncover past-embodiment details of your imprisonment and death for speaking and teaching spiritual knowledge, or for your inability as a healer to save the life of a child, your free-floating dread can be tied to a rational explanation.

Soul origin, whether EBS, IPS, or ARS, provides a reason for your degree of comfort based on sufficient earth-life experience or lack thereof and the ability to cope, easily or not, with human everyday energy and attitudes. Knowledge of yourself or a loved one as an IPS or ARS provides insight into your unease with crowds and intense energy, your child's difficulty learning with everyday methods, your susceptibility to stomach upset based on diet, and more. ARS are challenged to face the lack of love among humans for all people on our planet. It is a blessing, perhaps in disguise, to know from where your soul originates. Add in a dose of identifying your primary spiritual guide, who is ever present. When your soul, your HS, is your lead guide, then it is a sure thing you are an IPS or ARS.

Continuing to earmark your soul design: What are your passions in life now? Take hold of what gives you energy and a sense of *raison d'être* (reason for being). Then the picture of why you're in body has been created. What you love and provides excitement is your purpose. With your guides, a prebirth plan was set in motion for life today. For some, we have satisfied our original agreement. Only then do we have the option of developing additional fervent interests and actions, leading to life contract addendum.

Last, what are your soul themes across many lives and at present? The focal points of your human life—such as coping with grief, balancing the divine feminine-masculine, serving as a healer, and creating medical solutions for illness—are reflected in the responsibilities of your HS in the spiritual realm of your origin. *As above, so below; as below, so above* is the reality of your soul in the body and your soul in the higher realm. What you accomplish on earth is reflected in the role of your HS. Reciprocally, the responsibility of your HS is reflected in your human endeavors. Your HS is at work even when you are asleep.

Spiritual Practice: An Essential Component of Life

Spiritual practice is critical to maintaining your soul bond and receiving intuitive feedback from your HS and guides. Every day, take time in nature and listen with head and heart. Or, if you love candles, essential oils, music, or whatever floats your boat, utilize your ability to listen intuitively to what is vital in your life. Your guides never leave you. We need to remember to trust and listen.

JACK: An IPS Leads a New Earth Story

I'm in a Roman battle scene in a city. There's a doorway where I hide. My feet are in sandals, and I have a classic centurion look with a skirt and leather flaps. I have chest armor. My beard is dark and I have piercing blue eyes as a middle-aged man. As I watched, I saw a game of chess with my castle under siege. I'm some strategic ally to the king as his right-hand guy. The king is protected now by the guard. I snuck out to get a sense of what's happening. I'm to help create a strategic plan to counterattack from behind. I'm simply hiding and watching things.

No one sees me. The enemy thinks no one knows what's happening. They have no idea that we're already on to them. The king is safe as we prepare to circle and trap them. They won't even know what hit them.

I'm good at my job. This king is wise. At the same time, I play the brains for the king. He trusts me.

We're at a banquet toasting because we've outsmarted the enemy. A couple of women are trying to seduce the king, which is a different strategy to take the throne down. I'm not having any of it. I'm a watcher and must be always on.

I have a lot of affection for the king's two very loving kids with pure hearts. I'm the queen's brother. I deeply love my sister, who is a wise seer. My sister and I both have seer energy. In contrast, the king is a warm-hearted leader of the people. That's not my role, but he is effective in his role. The children are a boy and a girl aged thirteen and seven, who are a mixture of big hearts and savvy and intuitive intelligence.

It's years later on the coast, possibly the Amalfi Coast. I have gray hair and am retired. It's dusk as I sit and watch the ocean. People visit me for counsel on a combination of strategy and wisdom. I very much appreciate sharing my knowledge with these rising leaders.

I feel contemplative and know that life's end will come moderately soon. There is a connection with God in conversation as I sit near the water. It's like a life review and I have good feelings about my life. Also, I discuss the questions posed to me by others, and God offers perspective. I so appreciate the widening of my understanding.

When I retired and moved to the ocean, I had no idea this communication with God would arise. But the quieting of my busy life and duties led to just being able to hear the voice. It's about hearing the perspective on earth's activities. I sense a readying for my dying in the relative future.

I can see my body lying on the bed as I float above it. There are people around me. In scene one, I was in the drama. In scene two, I got some perspective on the drama. Finally, in scene three, I float above the drama. It's clear that earth beings are so wrapped up in whatever is going on in their lives. There's a hamster-wheelness with the daily drama of people's lives. Before I leave the scene of my passing, I realize that my sister, the queen, is the soul of a dear female friend. My beloved nephew in the past life is the soul of my very young nephew in life today.

As I travel home, I go via a light castle, past the aurora borealis, and then home, where my soul resides. Back now to my home planet. Each life on earth is just a little dip into the pool and then I journey home.

At home, there's a recharge that happens. Every time I come to earth, which isn't often, I have a depletion of life force. I must be in the field of home for refortification that both assists me in releasing the details of a past life and helps me progress in life today. There's a removal of the attachment to trauma in my visits to earth.

We're creating a new earth story. So before you can create a new story, you need to know that once you step out of an incarnation, you must delete the trauma of that life story. Then, and only then, can you usher in a new story, a new perspective.

• • • • • • •

Jack, an IPS, teaches us that we quickly become stuck on a hamster wheel in earth life. When we know we're souls living from one life to the next, we must let go of past-life trauma. Once our personal soul design research begins, creating a straightforward puzzle of various pieces, we can more easily map our present-life destiny. Our individual new story is reflected in a collective new story.

Things to Think About

- Think about how to utilize one of your skills more often.
- Trust that you are now conscious of the components of your soul design.
- Today, embrace your inborn qualities tied to thinking and feeling as you contribute to humanity.

Homework to Determine and Be Who You Are as a Perfect Being

1. Even if you're unsure, decide for now if you are an EBS, IPS, or ARS, and live each day with intention.
2. Take time each week to support someone close to you whom you believe needs to discover their soul design.
3. Use your journal daily to document your discovery of how your emotions and passions are tied to your soul design.

Acknowledgments

Gratitude begins with the innumerable soul regression clients over thirty years who were thirsty to know more about who they are as a soul.

Gratitude to Susan, the wise, detail-oriented, committed, caring interplanetary soul, our Ravenheart Center associate, whom we couldn't manage without.

Gratitude to my beloved husband, Earl, teammate, channel, life partner, and grounding force when I am in need.

Gratitude to Amy Glaser, editor at Llewellyn Worldwide, for agreeing to another book filled with soul regression material to support souls embodied on earth.

To Write to the Author

If you wish to contact the author or would like more information about this book, please write to the author in care of Llewellyn Worldwide Ltd. and we will forward your request. Both the author and the publisher appreciate hearing from you and learning of your enjoyment of this book and how it has helped you. Llewellyn Worldwide Ltd. cannot guarantee that every letter written to the author can be answered, but all will be forwarded. Please write to:

Dr. Linda Backman
℅ Llewellyn Worldwide
2143 Wooddale Drive
Woodbury, MN 55125-2989

Please enclose a self-addressed stamped envelope for reply, or $1.00 to cover costs. If outside the U.S.A., enclose an international postal reply coupon.

Many of Llewellyn's authors have websites with additional information and resources. For more information, please visit our website at http://www.llewellyn.com.